UNSURVIVABLE

Even in the darkest storm, always find your rainbow!

Sonya Hunter

29Eleven Ministries

Dedication

This book is dedicated to Kris, Adam and Conner

My love for them is never ending!

"Thank you, God, for the beautiful gift of Kris and Adam and for all the sweet memories. I will always hold these memories in my heart and soul. Memories that I will cherish for the rest of my life."

"Thank you, God, for the blessing of Conner. He is my precious miracle."

UN
SURVIVABLE

Even in the darkest storm, always find your rainbow
Published by 29ELEVEN MINISTRIES

Cover Design: Hunter Graphix, robbin@hgxsigns.com
Coach Writer/Author: Monica Madden www.monicaMmadden.com
Website Design: Impact Worship Solutions
eythan@impactsolutions.com

Printed in the United States of America
ISBN (paperback): 978-0-578-79703-8
10987654321
1st edition, October 2020

Registered with the Library of Congress
TX 8-915-055

Additional copies of this book can be ordered at:
www.amazon.com

Contact information:
www.29elevenministries.com
sonya@29elevenministries.com

Introduction

As you read my story, remember it is woven together by the love and grace of God…..

It was a beautiful spring morning. Sunshine, love and joy filled our home. My husband, Kris, was recently employed by the railroad and his new income was going to allow me to be what I always wanted, a stay at home mom. I had missed too much of the everyday joys of being with my two precious sons. There were so many wonderful possibilities just on the horizon for our beautiful family. Yes, sunshine filled my heart. Little did I know that this bright sunshiny day would become the darkest day in my life. My heart, my soul and my mind would be filled with a dense fog. The sunny day would soon become like a menacing thunderstorm, filled with a darkness I would not be able to comprehend.

Some names have been changed to protect their identity!

The Tragedy

My Family

Early one morning, my heart was so happy! I was counting down the days to my last day of work. Finally, I would get to be a stay at home mom. In the past year, I realized just how much I was missing my boys growing up. Kris's new job with the railroad was an answer to our prayer. With Kris's previous employment and my income, we could barely pay our monthly expenses. Though Kris would be traveling more, we were both looking forward to the opportunities his new job would give our family. We were even looking at the possibility of building a house.

As I continued getting ready for work, my mind raced with all the possibilities in store for our family in the months ahead. We had just celebrated our son Adam's sixth birthday and had surprised him with an inflatable water slide! I knew the boys would have fun sliding over the summer months. I would get to be home with them to enjoy their smiles and giggles as they made sweet memories. We hadn't even opened the box. The box was still sitting in our living room. I had made a promise to Adam we would set it up over the weekend.

As I finished getting ready, I could hear my nineteen-month-old son Conner talking to Kris. Kris had no idea what Conner was saying. Every few minutes I would listen to Kris laugh and say, *Is that right?* Then Conner would say, *Daddy*. Daddy was the only real word I recognized as I listened from the bathroom. Kris was such a good dad to our boys. His dad wasn't around as Kris was growing up. Kris was determined to be the best dad he could be to his kids. He loved playing with the kids on the floor and wanted to give them the best of everything. Kris wanted them to have the life he had only dreamed of having as a child. Adam was finally old enough to play T-Ball. Kris and my dad were going to coach the team over the summer.

We had many dreams for our family. We were excited about our upcoming Disney World trip later in the summer. I was making plans to surprise Adam with the opportunity to swim with the dolphins. He was going to be so excited when I told him! As I finished blow drying my hair, I couldn't help but smile at the thought of the look on his face when he found out. My dad and stepmom Donna had decided they would take all the grandkids to Disney World when they turned six. My dad loved making memories with his grandkids. We had even talked my sister into joining us with Caleb, my two and half-year-old nephew. We were going to have fun! My sister, Katrina, and I had tried talking about Disney World the night before. Adam kept interrupting us. We decided we would continue making plans over the weekend.

I peeked into the living room to check on Conner and Kris before saying goodbye to Adam. Conner was toddling around in his light blue pajamas. His hair was a mess. He was surrounded by what seemed like every toy in his toy box. The toys had found a new home on our living room floor. He looked up at me with his big smile and said, *mama*! I picked him up and gave him a big hug and kiss. I wanted to hold onto him. His wiggling told me he was ready to go again. Conner had lots of playing to do that morning. He loved to dance. I would have put on some music for him, but Adam was still asleep. Summer break had officially started today. I wanted to let Adam sleep in a bit.

Kris had been busy at the computer. He was checking his work schedule for the railroad. Kris was a conductor for a railroad company and would be getting on a train later that day. On Friday, May 19, 2006, I was thankful I could sleep in tomorrow. When Kris worked night shifts, I didn't sleep well while he was gone. His schedule changed from day today. He had to work fifteen days each month to get his base pay. He usually put in for more days so we would have extra money to put toward bills. Before I kissed Kris goodbye, I reminded him to put the paperwork in the mail for the life insurance the railroad offered their employees. He laughed and pulled me close, *You're not ready to get rid of me, are you?* he asked. I gave him a big kiss and hug and said, *You know I couldn't imagine life without you!* Kris was just three months away from being with the railroad one year.

I wiggled my way out of Kris's bear hug and headed in to check on Adam. He looked like a sleeping angel laying there. I couldn't believe how big he was getting. It seemed like yesterday he was a baby in my arms. He had finished kindergarten and would be heading to first grade in the fall. Adam loved Spiderman! He loved all superheroes. At the moment, Spiderman was his absolute favorite. Every time we would watch a Spiderman show, he would act out the parts just as if he was Spiderman himself. Complete with live web throwing action. I wasn't surprised that he was curled up in his Spiderman comforter. The only pajamas he would wear was his Spiderman underwear. When he was awake, he was full of life! Seeing him asleep and quiet was a rare moment for me. I leaned over and kissed him goodbye on his forehead. Moving away from his sweet face, I was thankful I didn't hit my head this time on the top bunk.

Walking out of the room, an unsettled feeling came over me. I wasn't sure why I felt that way. Life couldn't have been better. We had so much to look forward to in the months ahead. I think the feeling had to do with the conversation we had during dinner a few nights earlier. Adam was asking many questions about Heaven. Kris's mom had already passed away. Adam never had the chance to meet her. He wanted to go to Heaven to meet Kris's mom. I told him *it would be a long time before he would go to Heaven. Mama and daddy needed him too much.* Adam laughed and said, *I wouldn't stay, mama. I would just go for a visit and come back.* I knew he didn't understand that you didn't get the option to come back once you went to Heaven. I took one last look at him and told myself to stop worrying. I would see them for lunch.

As I gathered my things to walk out the door, I went back over Kris's schedule for the day. He told me he was going to pick up the t-ball uniforms at the Y in Ardmore. Since he didn't have to be at the railroad until later in the day, he and the boys would take me to an early lunch. Kris wanted to spend a little more time with me before he went to work that evening. I always loved our lunch dates. They gave me something to look forward to. We agreed on our favorite Mexican food restaurant in Madill. Growing up in Southern Oklahoma, we loved our Tex Mex!

I only had one more week to work before I would be home every day for lunch. Conner was tugging at my shirt and wanted me to pick him up again. When I turned to pick him up, he ran down the hall giggling. I chased him and scooped him up in my arms. I kissed him all over his face and told him I would see him in a little while. I went back over to Kris and pulled his face toward me. I kissed him one last time. Remembering he would be staying overnight in Fort Worth, I wrapped my arms around him and gave him an extra hug. I told him I loved him and headed to the car.

Driving to work that morning, I was listening to a Christian radio station. I was thinking about my last week of work. All of a sudden, the feeling of dread washed over me again. My heart started racing. I was nauseous. A sense of sheer panic coursed through my body. I remember having to calm myself down. Maybe it was because I only had a few days left of work. I loved my job, and I loved everyone I worked with. All twelve of us were like family.

The Accident

I worked for Red River Rehab in Madill, Oklahoma. Red River Rehab owned nursing homes and outpatient therapy clinics. I was a medical transcriptionist for a Physical Therapist, and I also had some secretarial duties. Arriving at work, I put aside the uneasy feelings I experienced during my drive and began my workday.

Around 9:30 am, Kris called me from the house and said, *Hey babe, we are about to head to the Y to pick up Adam's t-ball uniforms. Then we will head your way. Do you need anything else from town?* I replied, *I don't need anything. Call me when you are leaving Ardmore and heading my way.* Kris said he loved me and would see me in little while. I told him *I love you too.*

About an hour later, Kris called and said *Hey, we are heading your way. We'll be there in about thirty minutes.* I could hear Conner giggling in the background as Adam said, *I found your tickle spot.* Adam loved making Conner laugh. Adam loved his little brother so much and was very protective over Conner. The sound of the two of them in the background is a beautiful memory etched in my mind! I couldn't wait to be able to hear those sweet sounds all day long over the summer. I turned my attention back to the words Kris was saying and replied, *Ok, be careful. I love you.*

Busy at work, I looked down and realized it had been forty-five minutes since Kris had called me. I wondered what was taking him so long. He should have been here fifteen minutes ago. I picked up my phone to call Kris. No answer! I tried several times. Maybe ten calls. All unanswered. Uncontrollably the horrible, gut-wrenching feeling I had driving to work earlier immediately took over my body!

In a near panic, I started calling around. First, I called my dad's house. My stepsister Jennifer answered and told me that my dad and Donna (my stepmom) weren't home. Donna had been one of the boy's primary babysitters since she was retired. Adam had given her the nickname, "Nonna". Adam being the first grandchild, he got to be the one to name all of the grandparents. Jennifer did tell me that she had heard lots of sirens earlier. My dad's house was close to the highway Kris was traveling on. Jennifer said she was going to try to get in touch with dad or Donna.

I called Kris's brother, Jeff. No one answered at Jeff's home. I kept trying Kris's phone. Even though I knew, and yes, I knew, Kris would have called and told me he was making another stop.

I walked to my co-worker Sharon's office to tell her I knew something was wrong. I needed to drive to Ardmore. I was going to take the same route I knew Kris would have been driving. Just as I left her office, two police officers, Officer Fullingim and Officer Brown, walked in. I heard them ask, *Is Sonya McDougall here?*

Rounding the corner, Officer Fullingim immediately recognized me. We had attended high school and college together. He didn't know me by my married name.

I immediately saw the look in his eyes. A glimpse of devastation and sadness. He shifted back and forth as his eyes darted from me to my co-workers. His eyes reflected a look of fear and profound sorrow. I could sense he had something to tell me that I didn't want to hear. I searched his eyes again for hope. There was not even a glimmer. I knew he was about to deliver some devastating news as his eyes blinked to push back tears. I approached him with tears swelling up in my eyes. My heart was pounding, I knew something tragic had happened. I wasn't sure if I could handle it, I was terrified. My breaking heart knew the words that lingered just behind his solemn eyes.

He put his hand on my shoulder. Officer Fullingim patiently walked me to my co-worker Becky's office and sat me down. The entire office staff followed us in. Kneeling in front of me, he placed his trembling hands on my knees. He looked me straight in the eyes and informed me that

Kris and my boys were involved in an unsurvivable accident. With a shaky voice, Officer Fullingim told me Kris and one of my sons did not survive. He proceeded to tell me that my other son was at the Ardmore hospital and needed to be airlifted to Dallas, Texas. He said, *The situation is dire, and they need you to get there as quickly as possible. The doctor needs your consent to airlift him.* I looked at him and asked, *Which one of my babies is alive?* With a trembling voice, his eyes full of tears, he looked at me and said, *I don't know.*

My heart was just ripped from my chest. I can't describe the pain I was feeling. I tried to stand up. My legs buckled underneath me. My co-worker standing closest to me, Debbie, caught me and gently went down to the floor with me. She just held me. She tried her best to console me! I was crying so hard my lungs weren't getting enough air. I was getting lightheaded! The pain was unbearable, I felt like I was in a horrible nightmare! I wanted to wake up from it! There are no words to explain the hurt my heart and soul felt at that moment. Less than an hour before, I had told Kris for the last time I loved him. It would be the last time I would ever hear Kris tell me he loved me! Which baby had I kissed for the last time?

At that moment, I just wanted my mom.

The Hospital

As Debbie continued to hold me, I begged for the news to be false. I was only twenty-nine, I was too young to be a widow. We had many dreams for our family. For the first time in our married life, we were finally financially stable. My mind raced with many emotions and thoughts. I told myself to get up! I told myself I need to get to the hospital! With every thought willing me to move, all I could whisper back is, *I can't move.* I wanted to tell my co-worker I feel paralyzed. I wanted to scream, someone help me, please! Part of me couldn't move. I wanted the situation to be a dream, a horrible dream. This had to be a nightmare. I thought, maybe if I just sit here, I will wake up, and it will all go away. As my world spun out of control, I prayed, *God, please don't let this be true.* I started feeling very sick to my stomach. I felt like I was about to vomit. I had to try and make it to the bathroom. Crawling to the bathroom, I collapsed at the entry in front of the door. My co-worker's hands were on my back, letting me know I wasn't alone. I laid there, sobbing. Tears were rolling off my arm, puddling onto the floor. A memory flashed back from the week before. I was leaving the office kitchen. Walking to my office. I passed the entrance to the bathroom and was surprised when someone reached out and grabbed me. I turned around and there was Kris. He wanted to scare me. He embraced me with a hug and stole a quick kiss from my lips. That was Kris, always kidding around, always loving me.

Reality set back in and I started asking God. *God, can this be real? Did the police misunderstand the news? Why was this happening? We had a beautiful family! We had so many hopes and dreams. How would we survive financially without Kris? Which one of my babies was still alive? The following week was supposed to be my last week working. Would I still be able to quit? Did I truly lose everything precious to me? How would I ever survive this nightmare? I was supposed to stay at home with my boys!* My mind was racing. I somehow managed to quiet the questions flooding my mind. I got up off the floor and said, *I have to get to my baby!* Getting to the hospital became my mission. I had to get there. I knew my baby who survived would be scared. I knew he wanted his mama! He was all alone right now. I had to give him hope to keep living. I needed him and he needed me.

My boss, Erin, had called my mom. Later that evening, mom told me that when Erin called her. Mom had been checking out at Dollar General in Madill. A lady standing behind her could tell she had just received devastating news. Because mom looked upset, the lady wanted to make sure mom got home safely. She followed mom the entire twenty miles. Choc, my stepdad, was nervously pacing the driveway when mom got home. Mom also told me they had to drive through the site of the wreck. The road was still shut down and the police weren't going to let them through. Choc told the officer that was our son and grandsons. Graciously the police escorted us to the hospital. Mom said she closed her eyes as they drove by. She couldn't bear to see any part of the wreck.

Jennifer had already suspected the worst had happened. She called me back to check and see if I had found out anything. Erin had my phone and told her it was bad. She told Jennifer she needed to get to the hospital immediately. Jennifer said she can still remember hearing me screaming in the background. She called Donna to tell her she needed to get to the hospital because Kris and the boys had been in a bad accident. My dad was at a doctor's appointment. They couldn't reach him on his cell phone. They called the doctor's office to get through to him.

My co-workers knew that I was in no shape to drive to the hospital. I am still thankful for the office team I worked with. They were there to see me through the nightmare I was living. It was decided that Lisa would drive me to the hospital. Lisa was one of our RN's. She would be better equipped to handle things if I had a medical emergency on the way to the hospital.

My knees were trembling uncontrollably as my co-workers loaded me up in Lisa's vehicle. Lisa asked me if there is anyone else we need to call. I knew I had to break the news to my sister and Kris's siblings. *Lord, please help me, give me the strength to make these calls*. I didn't know where my purse was. Erin had given Lisa my phone. The first person I dialed was my sister, who lives in North Carolina. I couldn't stop crying. Katrina could barely understand me between sobs. If my name had not appeared on her phone, she probably wouldn't have known who was calling her. After about the fifth time of her saying, *Sonya, I can't understand you, what's going on*? I got frustrated and finally was able to scream out, *Kris and one of my babies are dead!* I then handed the phone to Lisa. I knew there was no way I could carry on a conversation with anyone. I was crying uncontrollably. Lisa told my sister she needed to come home immediately. We didn't know at the moment which of my babies survived the accident. She would need to make flight arrangements as soon as possible.

Driving down the road, Lisa called Kris's siblings. We found out Kris's sister and brother-in-law, Tracy and Eddie, had already been notified by the police. Eddie was formerly a police officer and the police department knew he would know how to get in touch with me. Tracy was trying to get to me before we left the office for the hospital, but she worked thirty minutes away. Unfortunately, she didn't get to me in time. Tracy told Lisa she didn't need to call the rest of their family because she had already contacted them.

When Lisa and I arrived at the hospital, there were so many family and friends there to support us. I couldn't figure out how all these people already knew about the accident. When we pulled up, the first person that came up to me was my pastor, Dr. Fannin and our Young Adult Minister, Todd Davison. Todd had just started at our church a few weeks before. Mom had called them on her way to the hospital. She knew I would need them there.

I could barely make out any faces, the entire room was a blur. Dr. Fannin escorted me to dad and Donna. They were the first ones to the hospital. I walked up to my dad, tears pouring down my face, and asked, *Which one of my babies is alive?* Nervously he replied, *Conner*. In agonizing pain, I crumbled to the ground. My head was swirling! My stomach ached, and my heart was crushed. I realized my precious Adam, my six-year-old son, was gone. I had just kissed his sweet face goodbye that morning before work.

If only I had known it would be the last time I would have seen him, I would have woke him up! I would have hugged him tightly! I would have never left his side that morning! I would never hear my sweet Adam's voice say, *I love you mama.* I would never be able to tuck him into bed! I would never be able to kiss him goodnight! I would never be able to feel him wrap his arms around me and hug me! I would never be able to see him grow into a man, to fall in love or get married. There were no words to explain the intense pain I was feeling. I was devastated. It was like someone took a knife and cut my heart right out of my chest. My beautiful son was gone. And I had lost Kris, my best friend, the love of my life, my husband, my lifelong partner, my rock. I kept repeating to myself, *God, please, take this pain away. Why did this happen? Why me? Why now? I just want to die, God! Take me too! God, please, I can't do this! I don't want to live anymore! How am I supposed to go on?* Both my husband and our six-year-old son were taken. And just like that, in a split second, my life would be changed forever.

Dad knelt beside me and said, *Sis, you need to get up and get to Conner. They need to airlift him to the Kids Hospital in Dallas.* With my body trembling, I reached to dad and he helped me up off of the floor. Not sure of Conner's state, but knowing his life was on the line, I tried to compose myself. I kept repeating to myself, *Be calm, Conner needs me. Be calm, don't panic!* Turning the corner into the ER trauma room, I could see so many people around Conner. I tried hard to focus on the Respiratory Therapist at Conner's head. Conner was intubated, had a c-collar around his neck, and had wires hooked up to him everywhere. He was just lying there lifeless. He was only wearing a diaper.

The Respiratory Therapist was using an Ambu bag to pump air into his lungs. This was how he was breathing. *Oh, my baby, my baby!* The Respiratory Therapist had Conner's life in her hands. Making my way to my lifeless Conner, the doctor stopped me to explain what was going on. Her words were lost in the surrounding noise. The only thing I heard was, *Conner has a spinal cord injury, he needs to get to Dallas immediately*. I kindly pushed her out of my way. I just needed to put my hands on my precious baby boy.

Seeing Conner like this was heartbreaking. Tears continued to pour out of me. I whispered into his ear, *Conner, I love you. I need you to fight hard. I need you to survive. Your mommy needs you more than ever right now*. I kissed him on his forehead. The doctor was rushing me. She was trying to get me to sign the paperwork to get Conner on the helicopter. I was frustrated! I just wanted one moment with Conner! I had to remind myself that Conner's life depended on getting to the Kids Hospital in Dallas. They needed to get him loaded and gone ASAP. Dallas had the best medical team and was best equipped for his injuries. I quickly signed the papers and asked the doctor, *Please let me see Kris and Adam. Please take me to them*. The doctor looked at me with a puzzled gaze and said, *They are not here*. I had not realized they died instantly and were not taken to the hospital.

Terrified for Conner, I felt like I was going to be sick! The doctors couldn't even assure me that Conner would survive the helicopter ride to Dallas. I was scared for my baby. I had already lost so much. I couldn't bear to lose Conner too. I prayed, *God, please help him, I can't lose Conner, please save him!* I turned to the medical staff as they were taking him to the helicopter. *Please let me ride with him! He's my only son! I need to be with him! I'm his mother! He needs me on that helicopter!* They responded, *Mrs. McDougall, We are sorry, but we cannot allow you to ride with us. Conner is critical, and you are not in a good state either. We are not equipped to take care of both of you if something happens to you on the flight. We have to be completely focused on Conner.*

I was scared, frustrated and hurting at the same time. I didn't know if Conner would survive the ride to Dallas. I was frustrated that I couldn't ride on the helicopter with him. I was hurting because I lost Kris and Adam. So many emotions flooded through my body at one time. I had to give someone else control over my son's life. I felt utterly helpless. I had to depend on someone else to save him, someone else to keep him alive, someone else to be with him if he died. Then I started praying, *God, please save Conner, please let him survive. He's all I have left.* As I was praying, a new panic hit me. How was I going to get to Dallas? The hospital was a two-hour drive. How would I be able to drive there? Where was my car? Where was my purse? Where were my car keys? Where was Kris when I needed him? *Please God, please wake me up, please let this horrible nightmare be over.*

Getting to Dallas

I was lost in my thoughts of turmoil and despair. Somewhere through the fog swirling in my mind, I heard my dad's voice calling out to me, *Sis, we need to get to Dallas. They don't want us to be too far behind them. The Kids Hospital won't be able to do anything without your consent.* Dad let me know he gave the helicopter pilot his cell phone number if something happened during the flight.

Several church members offered to drive us to Dallas. They were not sure any of us were in the right state of mind to drive. Dad assured them he could. He told them he wanted to make sure we had a vehicle while we were in Dallas. Leaving the hospital, I realized I needed all of us to be together. I stopped and grabbed my parents and asked them if we could all please ride together. We all piled in my dad's SUV with a nonverbal group consent and started the long drive to Dallas. Looking back to that day, I still don't know how my dad was able to drive us to Dallas.

A caravan of family and friends followed us to support us in prayer and love. The entire two hours to Dallas I cried my heart out. Still in total disbelief, I couldn't believe what was happening to me. How unfair my perfect little family had to go through such a tragedy. *Why God, why God, why are You allowing this to happen to me?* Sitting in the front seat, I was completely unsure about how I would survive this tragedy. Even surrounded by a loving family, I felt more alone than I've ever felt. I just wanted to wake up from the horrible, gut-wrenching nightmare.

On our way, mom was making phone calls. She asked, *Sonya, can you think of anyone that we should contact?* Immediately I responded, *Denver, Kris's best friend.* When Denver answered, he informed us that his mom had already let him know, and just like the rest of us, he was crushed and devasted. Whenever Denver was home, he always made a point to stop by the house. Kris and Denver would spend countless hours on the front porch solving all the world problems, sometimes well into the night. At the time of the wreck, Denver was in optometry school in Florida. To add to this heartbreak of losing his best friend, he was in the middle of his fourth year of clinical rotations and had to get permission to leave and come home.

My sister called to let us know they had found a flight. Katrina and her husband Robert, would arrive in Dallas between ten and eleven o'clock that evening. She told me she had reached out to several people and asked them to pray for Conner.

After the longest two-hour drive in history, we arrived at the Kids Hospital in Dallas. I only wanted to see and touch my baby. I needed to caress him and let him know that his mama was with him and not to be scared. As we pulled up to the emergency room, mom and I got out and hurried inside while they went and parked the car. Erin was walking in the hospital too. The nurse at the desk told me that only three people were allowed in the trauma area. Mom, Erin, and I went back. We had to stand outside the crowded room, the room was full of nurses and doctors. It was organized chaos of people with hoses, tubes, monitors and IV poles. The room was filled with the sounds of packages being ripped open. Doctors were barking orders and nurses were calling out vitals. Alarms were going off and monitors were beeping. All the while, my little baby boy was lying lifeless on a cold bed with nothing but a diaper on. I felt like I was watching a movie scene. It still didn't seem real. They were trying to keep him stabilized. I wasn't allowed to get close to Conner. I was horrified watching them work on him, knowing there was nothing I could do to help. My whole body was trembling and filled with fear. I had no clue what the future was going to hold for Conner.

The doctor informed us they were taking Conner back for a CT scan and MRI. The scans would give them a better idea of how threatening his injuries were. Mom, dad, and the hospital chaplain went with me to the imaging area. The hospital staff had us wait in an exam room across the hall from the testing area. My body was physically exhausted. The

Chaplain suggested for me to crawl up on the exam table and lay down for a minute. As I laid there, everything hit me like a tidal wave all over again. I longed for Kris to wrap his arms around me, to hold me, to tell me everything was going to be ok. I did not know it was possible to make as many tears as I had cried that day. My parents and the Chaplain loved and prayed over me the whole time. For the next 24 hours, the Chaplain never left our side.

The testing took forever, two-hours had already passed. Being anxious is an understatement. The Chaplain went to get an update. When he returned, he said, *They had to keep stopping the test. Conner kept crashing and the doctors and nurses had to keep reviving him.* I began praying frantically to God to please allow Conner to live. A nurse finally came in and told us that the MRI and CT scans were completed. We needed to go up to the eleventh floor ICU waiting room. As soon as they had Conner stable in his room, they would allow us back. I was getting frustrated. Anger was a new emotion that started to fill my already exhausted body. I just wanted to be with my baby! I knew they were working hard to keep him alive. Conner needed me and I needed him.

The ICU waiting room was filled with family, friends, co-workers, and church family. There was standing room only. I was shocked by the outpouring of love and support. So many people from home had driven the two hours to Dallas. They were waiting on us, ready to lend support in any capacity needed.

Someone offered me a chair. I wanted to hug everyone, but I didn't have the strength or words. I let my body melt into the seat. Our pastor bent down in front of me and offered me a sandwich from a food tray someone had brought. It was well into the evening hours and I had not eaten anything all day. I tried to choke down a couple of bites, but my stomach was in knots. It was tough trying to eat with my thoughts focused on Conner hooked up to machines. I wondered if he would survive. I was crushed knowing Kris and Adam were gone. I knew Dr. Fannin was right, I needed some fuel for my over-stressed body. I genuinely don't know how my body could function from all the stress it was under.

Another hour had passed and I still hadn't seen Conner. I started getting frustrated. I went to the desk and to the woman sitting there I said, *Look! It's been a long day! We've been here for several hours and I haven't got to see my son yet! I am not waiting any longer! I want to see my son now!* With a look of understanding and a quick headshake, she picked up the phone and made a call. *Mrs. McDougall is very upset that she hasn't seen Conner yet!* A minute later, a nurse came through the locked double doors and took our entire family back to Conner's room.

Walking to Conner's room, the sickening feeling started to rise in my body again. Stepping into Conner's room, the only thing my heart wanted was to get to Conner. In his long white coat, a doctor stopped us and said, *I have to warn you, you need to prepare yourself. Your son won't survive the night!* I fell to the ground and the tears started flowing all over again! On my knees, on the cold floor of the ICU room, I thought to myself, *if Conner dies, I do not want to live! I refuse to be here if my whole family is gone!* Suddenly, I felt my mom place her hands on my face. She had knelt in front of me to try and console me. With her eyes full of tears, mom lifted my head and made eye contact with me. Mom said, *Sonya, I need my baby girl to survive, I can't lose you too.*

At that moment, something clicked in me. I knew I needed to be strong because Conner needed me to be strong. I pulled myself up off the floor. I walked over to Conner and began to pray in his ear, *God is with you. Mommy needs you to fight hard. Mommy loves you so much! God, please let Conner survive through the night. Please prove these doctors wrong. In Your Son's most powerful name!* I stood there gently rubbing and caressing his arm for as long as my tired and over-stressed body would allow. Normally the hospital only allows four people in an ICU room at once. At this moment, they were allowing all of our family in the room. They didn't think Conner would survive through the night. They were allowing us to say goodbye to him.

I made my way to the couch, I collapsed on it, crying my heart out. I pleaded with God to save my child. I was hoping Conner couldn't hear me crying. I wasn't even sure he could hear anything. As much as I tried, the tears wouldn't stop falling. I was feeling completely heartbroken. My brother-in-law Tony came over to the couch. As he sat down, he picked my head up and placed it in his lap. Tony sat there and loved on me while I continued to cry. I longed for Kris, Adam and Conner more than ever!

Looking up from Tony's lap, I said to everyone in the room, *Please start prayer chains! I want everyone all over the world praying for a miracle for Conner! The next twenty-four hours will be very critical! I need him to survive through the night! Please get everyone you know praying for my baby!* Unfortunately, social media wasn't as big in 2006. We had to send out emails and call everyone we knew. One of my co-workers even contacted one of the biggest Christian radio stations in America and asked for people to pray.

Katrina had already been starting prayer chains. One of the people she called was Marilynn Blackaby, Henry Blackaby's wife. Henry is a Christian author and pastor. My sister had been roommates in college with Henry and Marilynn's daughter, Carrie. Katrina knew they had lots of faithful prayer warriors from all over and could get prayer chains started immediately. The Blackaby's had people around the globe praying for Conner through the night. I still have no clue exactly how many people were praying for Conner and me that night. I knew in my heart there had to be thousands praying for Conner's survival.

When my sister walked into the room shortly before midnight, she ran to me, and we cried together. By the time my sister had arrived, most of our family and friends had arrived at the hospital. Conner's Great Grandma, Kris's grandma Lebo, who lived in Tennessee, would be flying in the next day.

Sunlight beamed through the window. It was morning! God had heard our prayers! CONNER HAD MADE IT through the night! He was still alive, in critical condition and clinging to life, but none the less HE WAS ALIVE. The doctors were surprised. In their vast knowledge of medicine, they had said his injuries were unsurvivable. By the Grace of God and the prayers of his faithful, Conner did survive the night. *"For nothing is impossible with God!" Luke 1:37*

The Funeral

Making Funeral Arrangements

Another day dawned. I glanced over at my sweet boy. In the days since the accident, I woke up each morning hopeful the accident had just been a terrible nightmare. Looking over at Conner's little body with tubes running from almost every direction, it was such a contrast to our last morning together as a family. Many questions filled my mind, Would he be able to dance again? Would I ever hear the sound of his little feet running down the hallway with the swooshing of his diaper? I had barely left his side since we arrived at the hospital. The doctors had painted the worst picture possible for Conner's recovery. As I swept Conner's hair from his face and rubbed his right cheek, I told him how much mommy needed him and how much I loved him.

For a moment, I was lost in my thoughts of the sounds of Adam tickling Conner in those last moments before the accident. Then a nurse came in to check vitals and I was transported back to the reality of my situation. If only the doctors understood how much I had lost already, they wouldn't come in daily with such somber faces, always painting such a grim outcome for Conner's future. Don't they understand how much I needed hope at that moment? Despite what they said, my little Conner kept fighting.

In some ways, things had quieted down a bit around the hospital. Only immediate family remained with me. We still had others who would make the two-hour drive and bring food and snacks. It's incredible how something as simple as a basket full of snacks and rolls of quarters for the vending machine can be a lifeline of hope when you are in the hospital. Conner was still in very critical condition. According to the doctors, he could go at any minute. As we sat in Conner's ICU room, my mom looked over at me laying on the couch wrapped up in Kris' shirt and said, *Sweetheart, all of the funeral arrangements we can make from here are made. We have to go to the funeral home to finish up the last of the arrangements. I know you don't want to leave Conner, but this is something we have to do.*

I was so thankful to have my immediate family with me. I can't imagine how I would have accomplished writing the obituary and making funeral arrangements without them. I was grateful for all the people taking care of my house. I couldn't think about home at that moment. I had friends who took care of my dogs. One friend watered my outside flower beds, while another took all my inside plants and kept them watered at her house. My stepsister, Tracy, had all my mail forwarded to her house to take care of my monthly bills. Our hospital human resource worker, Sherry, who helped get families into the Ronald McDonald House and worked out home healthcare when patients were ready to go home, went way above and beyond her duties for us. She worked diligently with my parents to get the obituaries typed up, and she got all the paperwork faxed to the funeral home and health insurance companies. I was at such a loss in the horrible nightmare, two hours away from home. My Kris and Adam gone, my Conner clinging to life.

The railroad rented five hotel rooms for our family, which gave everyone a place to sleep. I took quick showers there, then would run back to the hospital. I didn't want to be gone any longer than I had to be. I couldn't bear the thought of leaving Conner's side at the hospital. Every moment I wasn't there with Conner was hard. Knowing I'd be leaving for six to eight hours to go back home to make the final funeral arrangements was going to be tough.

I had been so focused on Conner, I hadn't taken the time to grieve Kris and Adam. I felt like what I was experiencing was more than one person could handle at one time. For me to be strong for Conner, I could not afford to spend much time focusing on the heartache of losing Kris and Adam. I knew the moment we stepped inside the funeral home, the pain was going to wash over me. I knew I was going to be overwhelmed with grief. Up until that moment, I had tried to escape the thoughts of laying Kris and Adam to rest.

Sunday afternoon I kissed Conner on his head. I walked out of his room, dreading the ride home to finish up the funeral arrangements. I did not want to leave Conner's side. As I walked out of the building, I looked up to the blue sky and prayed, *God, please wrap Conner in your loving arms while I'm away. I can't handle something happening to him while I'm not here.* To help ease my mind, we had some of Choc's family and close friends stay at the hospital while we went to Ardmore.

I was exhausted, emotionally and physically. I could barely eat. My stomach was constantly tied in knots. My body was under so much stress. I was surprised that I could even function. I slept most of the way home. My body so desperately needed the rest.

Every time I had fallen asleep at the hospital, I had nightmares. I had the same dream over and over. I could see a scared look on Adam's face in Kris's truck. Adam would scream, *Mama!!Mama!!Mama!!* I kept waking up in a complete panic with my heart racing! Knowing I couldn't take much more of the dreams, I started praying very specific before dozing off. I would pray, *God, please cover me with Your grace.* After several days, the dreams finally stopped.

The Funeral Home

The funeral home was located across the street from my church. Pulling into the parking lot, tears once again started streaming down my face. I knew this was not going to be easy. I still couldn't believe I had lost Kris and Adam. I couldn't believe that I had to plan a funeral for them. Family members, close friends, and our pastor were already in the funeral home waiting for us.

Walking into the funeral home, my whole body began shaking. As the funeral director, Craig approached me. I was thinking, how am I supposed to do this? Thoughts kept coming. I can't do this! I don't want to do this! I was so angry! Why is this happening to me? Then heartbreak sank in. I couldn't explain what was happening inside me. I was racked with pain and a deep sorrow. What I was going through was too much for anyone to experience. I kept asking God, *Why are You allowing this to happen to my family?*

My body was shaking uncontrollably. I was led into a big room and sat on a couch. Craig sat on the coffee table in front of me, and in the kindest voice, he said, *We can go at your pace with all of this.* As I looked at him, tears streamed down my face, I replied, *Let's just get it over with!* Several of my family and Kris's family and lots of friends joined me in the room.

There were many options to go through. Craig began asking me many questions that flooded my mind all at once. They were questions I did not want to answer. Questions that seemed to be too soon in my life, in Kris' life and definitely in Adam's life! Do I want a family car to take us to the cemetery? Do I want a slide show at the funeral? Do I want a family night? Inside my mind was screaming NOOOO, I just want my family back! Out loud, I replied, *I don't know what I want! I don't want any of this! Let my family handle all these details! I don't care!* Craig then said, *Sonya, we need to go to the back and look at caskets.* Those words made my stomach turn upside down. The metallic taste of acid

30

filled my throat! The fear of what those words meant! So final! How was I supposed to pick out a casket for my six-year-old son? What parent would want to pick out a casket for their kid? I thought parents were supposed to die before their children.

As we walked into a room full of wooden and metal caskets, I noticed that a young worker was quickly removing all the prices. In my mind, I thought how strange. Clearly, I have to know how much the caskets are going to cost. I had no idea how I was going to pay for these funerals. *Craig, what is he doing?* I asked. Craig responded, *The people you work for are paying all expenses of the funerals. They do not want you to know any prices, so you will get what you want.* I was utterly blown away and beyond grateful. I closed my eyes and remembered, one thing that stands true forever, our God is amazing. He truly takes care of every need we have. We don't even have to ask him.

Lost in my own emotions, tears rolling down my face, my thoughts were of my sweet Adam laying inside one of these caskets. I kept thinking, this can't be real! Donna directed me over to a pearl white set that we could choose for both Kris and Adam. I sadly nodded ok to them. I started having trouble breathing. The room was shrinking in size, darkness was setting in. I began to feel claustrophobic. I knew I had to get out of that room immediately.

Quickly walking out of the room, I found a chair and sat down to compose myself. Looking up, I saw Craig walking by. I stood up and said, *I want to see Kris and Adam.* Craig's eyes grew large, and his chin dropped. The look on his face told me that seeing them was a bad idea. Composing himself, he looked me in the eye, and with an uneasy voice, he told me their bodies were not prepared for me to see. With all the strength I could muster at that moment, I responded, *I am not leaving until I see them!* Knowing many people would be going to the funeral home to pay their respects, there was no way I would allow anyone to see them before I did! Dr. Fannin was standing nearby and heard my request. He touched my shoulder and quietly asked, *Are you sure that you want to see them before they have them prepared for you?* Looking at him with tears welling up in my eyes, I said, *I have to see them!* I then stated, *We would not be having a family night. When I get back to Conner, I will not leave until the day of the funerals!* I would not be persuaded. The decision was made to let me see their bodies. Craig turned to the friends and family standing around me and stated he would only allow me, my parents, and Dr. Fannin into the back. Letting family see an unprepared body wasn't something they usually allowed, but they made an exception this time. I didn't care what exception was made, as long as I got to see Kris and Adam.

The First Viewing

Craig stopped us in the hallway. He informed us he needed to cover up Kris's head before we came in. I had no idea of the extent of the accident. I hadn't asked any questions about the wreck. The only thing I knew was that Kris had rear-ended a dump truck. I wasn't worried about the details at that moment. My main concern was Conner surviving.

Stepping back into the hallway, Craig holds the door and says to me, *Due to Kris's injuries, don't touch the top of his head or chest.* I couldn't even begin to imagine how bad Kris was going to look. As the door open to the room where the bodies were kept, the cold air surrounded my body. My eyes were suddenly drawn to the large word on the wall in front of me "MORGUE". I completely froze. All I could do was close my eyes and pray. *Jesus, Jesus, Jesus, please help me, Jesus*!

When I opened my eyes, I saw Kris and Adam lying on stainless steel tables with sheets draped over their bodies. Sickness, heartache and indescribable pain hit me all at the same time! I was immediately drawn to Adam! I wanted to pick him up and hold him. I'm still unable to describe what I felt at that moment. Only a mother who has lost a child knows what I was feeling. The feeling of wanting to comfort and hold your baby, and at the same time realizing you will never be able to again. I cried out to him, I told him I was so sorry and that his mama loved him! Uncontrollably the word '*NO*' kept leaving my mouth! This couldn't be real. This couldn't be my baby who grew inside my body. He had the sweetest spirit about him. He had a bright future! He was my boy! He was my Adam! He can't be lying dead on this cold metal table! How could I possibly go on living! Uncontrollably crying, I began screaming, *NO, I can't do this. I can't go on without you!* I felt so much heartache. The excruciating pain overtook me.

I turned to where Kris was lying. I only had a few steps to walk, but it seemed like it took forever to get to Kris. I was horrified by the way he looked. Even with the white sheet covering him, I could tell that something was really wrong with his head and body. He was so swollen. It didn't look like him at all. I wanted to love on him. I wanted Kris to sit up and put his arms around me! I needed him! Kris was my rock and my best friend! I needed him now more than ever! I wanted him to tell me to be strong, but he couldn't. The man that held my heart and loved me unconditionally was lying in front of me on a cold silver platform. How was I supposed to move on in life without him? All I could do was cry out in anger. My heart was breaking! *Oh God, this is too much! I can't handle it! I can't do it! I'm not strong enough! This is unsurvivable!*

Knowing I was close to my breaking point, Dr. Fannin quickly stepped up, wrapped his arm around my shoulders, and slowly walked me out of that cold, lifeless room. Looking into his eyes, I saw that he had tears streaming down his face. As we walked out into the hallway, my body betrayed me. The toll from all the raw emotions I had experienced over the last two days forced my legs to buckle, and I crumbled down to the cold hard floor. I couldn't get up. I just laid on the floor, crying and screaming out for Adam, my sweet baby! Losing my husband was horrifying, but losing my child is an excruciating pain I wouldn't wish upon anyone. I genuinely believe there is no greater pain. As parents, we are conditioned to believe that we are supposed to die before our children.

Dad came over and tried to get me off the floor, he tried to calm me down. Blinded by pain and anguish, I was unaware that another family had entered the funeral home while we were back in the morgue. They had just lost their loved one too. Dad and Denver finally got me up and into a private room where the rest of my family and friends were. As I was seated on one of the couches, everyone began loving and praying over me trying their best to help subdue some pain. My parents met with Craig and finished up the remaining details of the funeral. Leaning over, I laid on the couch and continued to cry my heart out. I thought, why couldn't it have been me? Why did it have to be Kris? Why isn't it me in Heaven experiencing the streets of gold? Why do I have to be the one here dealing with all the pain and suffering? I am not strong enough to live through this!

Then I started feeling guilty, this is all my fault! Why didn't I just go pick up the T-ball uniforms? Why did I send Kris to get them that morning? The boys and I were supposed to go to town later in the evening. We had planned to attend Adam's best friend Clay's birthday party that night. Why didn't I pick up the uniforms on the way to the party? I could have avoided this whole nightmare. None of this would have ever happened to us! This is all my fault! Now remorse was adding an entirely new stress to my already weak mind and body. Guilt!

My parents were finally finished with the remaining parts of the funeral. At long last, we were able to leave the funeral home. As nice and patient as the funeral home workers were, I was so relieved to finally leave that place of death! I was so ready to get back to Conner! Before heading back to Dallas, we all needed to stop by our homes to gather up personal belongings that we might need while we stayed at the hospital. I also had to go to my house to show Tracy, Kris's sister, where our family pictures were because she was putting together the slide show for the funeral.

The Accident Spot

I walked out and got in the back seat of my mom's car. Choc was driving with mom upfront, and Katrina was in the back with me. Pulling out on the street, I asked out loud, *How can anyone survive something like this, especially without God in their life?* I had thrown so many emotions at God. I was angry at Him because he now had Kris and Adam. I was sad, and I was disgusted. I wondered why God had allowed this to happen. I questioned why he had allowed this to happen to me? With tears falling, mom said, *It would be incredibly difficult. They wouldn't have the hope we have in Jesus.* Katrina and I both voiced how grateful we were that our parents had taken us to church growing up. I know I wouldn't have made it without the hope that Kris and Adam were Heaven. Adam was getting to meet his grandma, and Kris was getting to see his mom. I missed them terribly, but I knew they were in the presence of Jesus. Even though I had times when I was angry at him for allowing this to happen, I didn't stay angry for long. God understood all of my feelings. He is a BIG God! He gave us these feelings as humans. He understands because God had to watch His own Son go through an excruciating death! I knew God had been with me over the last couple of days.

The thought that we would be driving by the accident spot never crossed my mind. I wasn't even sure where the exact location was. As we drove down the highway, we saw our neighbor Roger, putting up a five-foot white wooden cross on the side of the road where the wreck had happened. Uncontrollably crying, I sank deeper into my seat. Choc pulled the car over. We were all feeling the sharp pain of the loss. Being there in that exact spot brought the nightmare back into reality. I thought, this is the place my family died. I will have to drive by here every time I go to town. Why did this happen on a road I have to drive on? How am I supposed to drive by this reminder of my family's death all the time?' I asked Choc to please go, I couldn't stand being there one more second.

Home

Pulling into the driveway, my puffy eyes started to fill with tears. The sweet memories sneaked out of my eyes. I felt like time had stood still. Along the driveway was Adam's bike, the boy's cars and a lone superhero figure. I was certain Spiderman had been saving the day in Adam's imaginative world. Seeing all of their toys and knowing life would never be the same, the tears streamed down my face! This was our home. Our home was so full of our happy memories. As I made my way into the house, my tear-filled eyes were suddenly drawn to Adam's giant waterslide. There it was, still sitting on the living room floor in the box. We had just got the slide for his birthday nine days before the accident! Nine days before he was taken away from me! Only nine days ago, I thought my life was perfect. Laying across the kitchen chair was Adam's Spiderman costume. He had probably changed out of Spiderman costume just before they left the house. As I walked through what had been my happy home, I pictured the boys chasing each other and giggling. I thought I would never have happiness in my life again. Will anything ever be the same? At the moment, it seemed impossible that I would ever have true joy again. My sister and mom followed me as I walked towards Adam's room. Opening the door and stepping in, grief overcame us. We all cried together. After several minutes passed, they asked if I would like a few minutes alone in Adam's room. I told them yes. I needed a moment to be alone in the last place I had seen my baby boy.

Sitting alone in agony and pain, I was overwhelmed. How is my baby truly gone? I curled up in his spiderman comforter and laid on his bed. I grab his stuffed dalmatian dog that he slept with, the dog smelled just like him. I pictured how every night, as I was tucking him in, he would wrap his arms around me and say *I love you, mama!* What I would have given to hear him say those sweet little words to me again.

I finally made myself get up. Adam's pillow was covered in my tears. I was ready to get back to Dallas. My other baby needed me! My eyes drifted to the birthday gifts of new clothes that would never be worn and toys that would never be played with. As much as I wanted to stay in Adam's room with his comforter wrapped around me, I forced myself to go to my bedroom to grab some clothes. I did my best not to focus on anything of Kris's. I was already so miserable. I had already dealt with way more pain than I needed to for a lifetime. I quickly left our bedroom and made my way to the living room. I needed to show Tracy where all of our family pictures were. I told her to go through them and pick the ones she wanted. There was no way I was emotionally ready to go through photos at that moment. All I wanted to do was get back to Conner.

Back at the Hospital

I got into the mom's car's back seat and laid my head against the window as we headed back to Dallas. I wanted to sleep on the way back to the hospital, but sleep wouldn't come. The quietness of the drive and the reality of what had been lost, once again surrounded us in a blanket of sadness. Everyone was lost in their own thoughts. We were all trying to process what we had just experienced. Pulling into the hospital's parking garage, we knew we had to clear our minds so we could focus on Conner. Putting the car in park, Choc turned to us in the back. *I want to pray over us before we go back in,* he said. Choc prayed for guidance and peace for our family. He prayed for God to grant us wisdom and strength for all the unknowns that stood before us. With a simple Amen, we got out of the car and made our way back to the ICU.

I worried that Conner was scared while we were away from him. We entered the giant train room in the foyer of the hospital. I thought, in another time, Conner would have loved to see the trains. The elevator ride up to the twelfth floor seemed like it took ages. When we got to Conner's room, I let out the breath I was holding in. Conner was still alive! *Thank you, Jesus*! I knew that I could have been planning a funeral for all three of my loves. I knew Conner was very critical and had a long road ahead of him. I knew along with myself, numerous other people were believing and claiming a miracle for Conner's life!

The nurse on duty told me Conner remained stable with no major issues while we were gone. I longed to hold my baby, but I knew I couldn't right now. Conner looked so small lying in the hospital bed. He had tubes and wires attached all over his body. Finding a way through all the tubing and wires, I nestled my head against Conner's face. I wanted to feel his skin against my skin. I wanted him to know I was there! I wasn't allowed to stay there for long, it was time for the nurse to do her assessments. Sitting there, I couldn't stop staring at Conner. I was afraid to take my eyes off him. I think the trauma of seeing Kris and Adam, scared me knowing how critical Conner was. Would I lose him as well?

Letters to Kris and Adam

The night before the funeral, I walked down to the chapel in the hospital. Personal time had been rare since the accident happened. I needed to be alone with God. On the way down, I silently prayed that no one would be in the chapel. Opening the doors to an empty room, a sigh of relief escaped my lips. The room was small but yet peaceful. By the door was a small table with paper and pens. There were three wooden pews with orange padding on each side of the room. I found myself sitting down on the front row. For several minutes, I just sat and stared at the wooden cross on the wall. I kept thinking about Mary and how she must have felt watching Jesus, her son beaten and hanging on a cross.

With tears falling from my eyes, I started talking directly to God, *Why do I have to endure this horrible path I am on?* Being mad and even a little jealous that God had Adam in Heaven, I continued, *It's not fair that you got Adam, he's supposed to be here with me! I'm not supposed to lose my child, a parent is always supposed to die first. We were good Christian people. Kris and I loved each other deeply, we loved our boys with our whole hearts. This isn't fair to my family! How do I ever get past this? It is hard enough to lose one family member, but to lose two at the same time. My husband and my son are gone, and my baby boy, barely clinging to life. This is way too much for me to handle!!* At that point, anger had overcome my sorrow. I stood up and began pacing the room. I kept verbally repeating the word "*why*". Deep in my spirit, I was reminded that children are gifts from God. Adam was his before he was mine. Knowing it didn't make my pain any easier. Adam had been God's gift to me for six years. I would have given anything to redo those six years. I would have spent more time with Adam. I wouldn't have taken for granted a single minute or allowed myself to get frustrated when he interrupted me. My emotions were all over the place, I was a basket case. I was sad, worried, hurt, numb, jealous and mad. I felt like there was a massive void in my heart, the intense despair I felt was maddening. There was nothing I could do to control my feelings, the only thing I knew to do was to fall to my knees and cry out to God.

Sometime later, I felt a strong urge to write letters to Kris and Adam. I would write down everything I wanted to tell them, just like they were standing in front of me. I would fold the letters up and put them in the caskets to be buried alongside my guys. Getting up from the ground, I walked to the table at the chapel entrance and grabbed a few pieces of paper and a pen, then I sat back down on my pew. I started with Kris' letter first.

With a trembling hand, I began to write, Dear Kris….

I told my husband everything that was in my heart. I thanked Kris for how good he was to me. I wanted him to know he was such a gift to me. I also wanted to apologize for the many times I took him for granted. The letter was a personal secret between a loving wife and the man she would love forever. The letter was everything that I didn't get to say before he was gone. The paper was stained with my tears, and the ink was running. While writing the letter, so many memories flooded back to me. I would never forget the day I came home from work, and Kris was on the floor playing with Conner. When I walked over to pick Conner up, he said his first word, *DaDa*. I was crushed. I had been able to stay home with Adam, and his first word was *mama*. I immediately felt mom guilt for having to work and not staying home more with the boys. The boys spent the day with either Kris when his schedule allowed or with my parents. Kris gave me a hard time, but he was upset, knowing I was crushed. He spent the next week teaching Conner to say, "mama". About a week later, when I came home from work, Kris gave me a big hug and said he had a surprise for me. He brought Conner over to me, and with a big smile on his face, he told Conner to tell me the new word he had learned. Conner ran over to me, grabbed hold of my leg, and said, *Mama!* I was so surprised and amazed Kris had taught our boy how to say, Mama. He was such a good husband and dad! I couldn't imagine how I would be able to do life without him. I pulled the paper up and kissed it just before folding it.

On a new sheet of paper, I started my second letter, My baby boy Adam….

I wrote how I wished I could've watched him grow up into a young man, watched him get married, have grandkids. I felt like I was robbed of all the joy I was supposed to be experiencing. I kept thinking over and over, did they know how much I truly loved them! Did I do enough to show them all my love, because my love for them ran so deep! I am sure this is something everyone questions when they lose a loved one. I think Adam's letter was the most difficult in some ways, grief was taking over, and I did all I could to see through my tears. Adam's life was just beginning. He would never get to do all the things we dreamed of experiencing with him. I shared with Adam how precious he was to me and how I will always remember holding him for the first time. I told him how much his dad and I loved him and how proud we were to be his parents. He was such a great big brother. I was in pain; Conner wouldn't have his big brother as he grew up. I continued to write and thought about how Adam had such a big imagination. When he came home from Kindergarten, he would run into the house, take off his clothes, and put on his Spiderman Costume. He loved all superheroes, but he especially loved Spiderman. He would run around the house, flinging his imaginary webs and saving the world. As he rescued the pantry from the dreaded death spider, which I asked him to step on for me, he would cast his webs and fly off again. At suppertime, he stopped attacking villains only long enough to eat up the macaroni and cheese I had placed on the table and try hiding the vegetables he wasn't as fond of eating. When I referred to him as "Adam," he would quickly remind me, his name wasn't "Adam" his name was "Spiderman"!

I was numb and weak after writing the letters. I sat there a few minutes longer in complete silence, questioning how I would move forward in life? Writing the letters had drained me emotionally. I wished I could just stay in the chapel. The chapel was so peaceful, and I didn't want to face what was coming in the days ahead. I felt so alone, but I felt like God was sitting beside me while I was in the chapel. Like a pinprick to the brain, reality set back in. I had been away from Conner for over an hour and needed to get back to him. Somehow, I found the strength to get up and head back to the ICU.

The Day of the Funeral

There are days in life that are so good you wish you could relive them over and over. There are days that are bad, and you just want to forget them. Then there are days you wish just didn't exist. I now own two of those days. May 23, 2006, is the day the love of my life and our sweet six-year-old son were laid in their final resting place. The pain I felt on that Tuesday afternoon was only rivaled by the pain of hearing about the wreck four days earlier. I knew I would need extra strength to get through today. The funeral made everything so final and ended my love story way too soon. I walked across the room to Conner and rubbed his sweet head, and told him to stay strong for me while I was away. I told him I loved him and would be back soon. I told him he wouldn't be alone. My eyes were swollen and sore, my lungs were tight, my body was tense, and my mind was scattered. What I dreaded the most was seeing my oldest son lying in a casket. This would be an experience I wasn't sure my strong faith would even let me endure. I wouldn't wish this pain on anyone. Burying my son seemed unsurvivable.

I knew their spirits were separated from their bodies. In a blink, they were in Heaven rejoicing with God. The sheer thought of seeing them in a casket made my stomach turn inside out.

A sunny and very windy Tuesday, winds were gushing up to twenty miles an hour. I had one son very critical in ICU, another son lying in a casket and his body waiting to be buried. I would have preferred to be the mom sitting, praying and crying for her nineteenth-month-old son in ICU. On that day, I had to be the mom who would bury her son along with the man who held my heart. I was so scared to be two hours away from Conner when he was in such a critical condition. I kept thinking, what if Conner dies while I'm away? Would I ever be able to forgive myself? While we were attending the funeral, some of our close friends and a few family members stayed in Dallas with Conner.

The drive home was miserable and seemed to take forever. I prayed for God to protect Conner and give me the strength I needed to live through this dreadful day! I was so weak and so broken. I wasn't sure how I was going to be able to stand on my own two feet! I knew I had to rely on God's strength to carry me through this day. I kept repeating the Bible verse 1 Chronicles 16:11 KJV, "Seek the Lord and his strength; seek his face continually. I knew my only option was to look to God. Only He understood, and only He could supply me with the strength I needed.

Amy, my close friend, was back home, getting things ready for me. She asked me what I wanted to wear. She was planning to iron my outfit for me. The first thought I had was to wear one of Kris's shirts, so I could feel like he was close to me. Several days before, Tracy, my sister in law, had brought me one of Kris's recently worn OU t-shirts to the hospital. His shirt smelled just like his cologne. People at the hospital probably thought I was crazy. I carried his shirt around with me the entire time.

I told Amy to get the black dress with the blue flower print on it. It was the same dress I had worn to church on Mother's Day, six days before the accident. I'll always remember Kris telling me how beautiful I looked that morning. I had Kris's wedding ring on a gold chain necklace. Wearing Kris's ring around my neck made me feel like he was close to my heart. I needed to feel as close to him as I could. I was about to live the unimaginable. I desperately wished I could feel his arms around me. I wanted to hear him tell me everything was going to be okay. When he would wrap his arms around me, I always felt safe. At this moment, I didn't feel safe.

The Funeral

I grew up at First Baptist Church. I loved my church and church family. We were raising our boys in the same church I grew up in. I was ready for that day to be over. I did not want to face anyone! I realized so many people wanted to love on me. They wanted to be there for me, but I knew emotionally I couldn't handle it. Pulling into the church parking lot, I told my parents I needed to see Kris and Adam one more time. I went over to the funeral home across the street. Inside the funeral home, I requested to be left alone with my two guys for just a few minutes. Different members of my family kept peaking in the room. They were concerned. I had barely eaten in days, and my body was weak. I felt like I was going to pass out.

I privately wanted to read the letters I wrote to them. I knew in my heart they couldn't hear me. I needed to read the letters out loud for myself. After I finished reading the letters, I placed each letter under their hands. I just wanted to find a spot and curl up on the ground beside the caskets and lay there. Dad came into the room and asked me if I was ready to walk back over to the church. *No, I was not ready for any of this!* What I wanted to do was run up and down the street and scream at the top of my lungs. Unfortunately, running up and down the street screaming wasn't an option. I turned and started to walk towards him. Every part of me felt so weak, I struggled even to stand. Dad and Uncle Dean got on either side of me and held me up. We headed over to the fellowship hall of the church. My eyes and face were so swollen from crying, and my head was pounding. Friends and family had gathered in the fellowship hall to eat the lunch our church members had prepared.

I told dad and my uncle I didn't want to go in the fellowship hall. I wanted to say thank you and show my gratitude to everyone, but I wasn't physically ready to face people. They understood and took me to the church library. Dad and Uncle Dean were so gentle and tried their best to comfort me. I sat there, trying to compose myself enough to make a brief appearance in the fellowship hall.

As time was getting closer for the funeral to start, I made my way into the Fellowship Hall. The first person I saw was Judy Fannin, our pastor's wife. I walked up, and she greeted me with a hug. She told me she wished she could sit and rock me. Oh, how I wish she could have at that moment. I was looking around the room for Mike, one of my co-workers but more like a big brother to me. A big hug from him sounded good. We constantly taunted each other at work, just like a sister and brother would do. He could always find a way to make me laugh. I asked Erin where he was, and she said he was already in the sanctuary. He was one of our pallbearers. Unknown to me, Erin went and got him. I watched him walk through the double doors, and we both started crying. He quickly walked over and hugged me. The little things, something as simple as a hug, can give us comfort. Even if just for a minute.

Craig, the funeral home director, walked in. I knew the time had come. If I wouldn't have had on dress shoes, I think I would have run away. The indescribable pain and uncontrollably crying was back. How could my body or spirit take any more of this heartache?? Burying my husband and son would have been unsurvivable if it had not been for people lifting me up in prayer! Only by the Grace of God was I still standing.

The fellowship hall is in a different building than the main church. We had to walk across the parking lot to get to the church. Mom and Choc were on my left side, and dad and Donna were on the right side of me. They told me the church was completely packed. They continued telling me some so many people loved us, and they were there to show their support. There was standing room only in the main sanctuary, and the balcony was completely full.

Our family started lining up in front of the big wooden doors to the sanctuary. Suddenly weakness once again filled my body. My legs were numb, and my body was trembling. Heartache swept over me again. Tears covered my face, the soaked tissue I had in my hand couldn't dry anymore. I looked at my parents and begged them to let me leave. With a trembling voice, I rambled, *Just take me back to Conner, I can't do this, I don't want to do this, please don't make me stay!* Just as the words escaped my mouth, the big wood doors opened, and once again, I was slapped back into reality. All four of my parents held me up as we made our way down to the front of the church. Walking down the aisle, everything to my left and right was blurred out of my vision. I had tunnel vision, and all I could see were the white pearl caskets sitting at the front of the church. The words *my baby, my baby* began to spill from my lips.

Adam's casket was so small compared to Kris's. How is it possible my little boy was lying in this casket? It had just been thirteen days since we had celebrated his sixth birthday. I know my cries were so loud. The scene unfolding in front of me was unbearable and unthinkable. I've always heard people say they felt like they could die from a broken heart. For the first time, I fully understood what the phrase meant. I was so focused on Conner fighting for his life, I hadn't grieved Kris or Adam. I was scared. What if I had to do this all over again with Conner. No one was sure what the next few days would bring. But I knew I couldn't relive this nightmare. If Conner didn't make it, the next funeral would have two caskets too!

My head was pounding because of all of the crying and sobbing. How was it possible for my body to produce so many tears? The funeral started, music played, and people spoke. I was oblivious to everything. I could only focus on the caskets! I just kept asking God, *Please let this be over*! The only thing I do remember, Amye singing the song *I Can Only Imagine*. In my mind, I sang every word. That was one of Adam's favorite songs. He made us play it over and over. The song paints such a beautiful picture of what they were experiencing in Heaven. I was so thankful the service was recorded so I could go back and listen to all the wonderful things others had said about Kris and Adam. I was so grateful for Dr. Fannin's' message. The memories shared of Adam from Mrs. Marshall and Mrs. Jill, and for Denver standing up and telling Kris's stories touched my heart. Our family asked our pastor to give the plan of salvation at the end of the funeral. If watching me bury my husband and son wasn't proof that tomorrow is never guaranteed, then I didn't know what was. I was so thankful I knew Kris was saved! The only peace I had was knowing one day we would all be together again!

The time I dreaded came, time to open up the caskets for viewing! As I watched the people from the funeral home open the caskets, my heart crushed into a million pieces. Dr. Fannin walked over to me and said, *just focus on the slide show*, a slide show of our family. My mind kept thinking, I'll never again see Adam run through the house, pretending to be Spiderman and shooting his web at us. Our home was now going to be empty and quiet. The thought of going back to our home without my family made me sick!! All I could do was lay my head on my dad's shoulder and cry into his arm! I just wanted the day to be over!!

As everyone finally made their way out of the church, they let me have one last moment with Kris and Adam. As I walked up to my little boy, I cried and cried. I longed to pick him up and hold him. I told him I loved him more than he could have ever known. I told him I was so sorry this happened to him, and I would never get over losing him! I leaned down to kiss his forehead, and all I could do was thank God for allowing Adam's face to be unharmed! He looked perfect!

As I walked over to Kris, my eyes were almost swollen shut at this point. He was swollen from all the injuries he sustained in the accident. He didn't look like the love of my life lying there. They put an OU hat on him to try and hide the damage, but the hat didn't help much. He definitely took the brunt of the accident. I wanted him to get up and put his arms around me to make me feel safe again! I needed him more than ever. How was I ever going to survive without him? I told him I loved him, and he would always have a special place in my heart that only belonged to him!

The Pallbearers were in the foyer, allowing me to have my time. As the funeral home director ushered them back in, I watched as they closed the caskets for the final time. I thought about how I would never again see their human bodies. We followed behind the pallbearers. I couldn't stop thinking about why this happened to our family.

As we made our way out of the church, I remember looking out over the parking lot and seeing all of the people showing their support. Our pastor had told everyone during the funeral as much as I would love to hug everyone, I couldn't handle it emotionally. I wish I could have handled all of the hugs but looking out and seeing how many people were there to support us was like one giant hug in itself.

Physically and emotionally, I was completely drained! It took everything I had to even stand up at that point! Only by the grace of God and all the prayers going up for me was I able to stand! All I wanted to do was get back to the hospital.

As our family cars made their way from the church to the cemetery, we were amazed at our community's love and support. People had lined the route and were standing in silence to honor Kris and Adam. The tragic accident impacted our entire community, partly because both Kris and I were so young. We were a young married couple at the end of our twenties, happy with two very young kids. Their lives ended too soon. The whole community struggled to wrap their heads around how life could end so abruptly and so unexpectedly.

The Cemetery

The Cemetery we chose to lay them at rest was near a train track. Kris's brother Jeff was able to find lots near the tracks. He knew Kris would have loved the trains, and when I went to visit, I would be reminded of Kris. As we pulled up at the cemetery, I didn't want to get out of the car! This was an image I didn't want to remember. As I made myself get out, the wind was blowing so hard! I was thankful for the sunshine.

As I made my way to the tent, I was amazed at the number of flower arrangements circling the tent. There were flowers in so many beautiful colors, way too many to count. I found my seat as quickly as possible. I was so tired and ready for the day to be over. I left room on either side of me for my parents. I knew they would find their way to me. As I sat there looking at the flowers sitting on top of the caskets, I felt as if I was burying all my dreams with Kris and Adam. Our dream for a new house. Our dream to go to Disney with Dad and for Adam to swim with the dolphins. The happy moments we were going to have over the summer on Adam's new waterslide. I was burying first day of schools, Middle School dances, learning to drive, prom and High School graduation. I was burying growing old with my first love. I wasn't just burying my family, I was burying everything we had hoped for. I was burying all the moment's parents were supposed to have with their kids. I was burying the dream to see my son grow up, get married and have a family.

In that moment, I had no idea what Conner's life would be like when he recovered. As I sat there lost in my thoughts, I also whispered to Adam and Kris *I love you*. Our pastor was sharing a short Bible reading. I felt my Dad put his arm around me. He knew I needed him at that moment. I reached up and felt Kris's ring again. I remember the day I put the ring on his finger and said, *I Do!* What a great day of celebration that was for us. My pastor, Dr. Fannin, had also led that ceremony. Tears streamed down my eyes as I thought of our wedding day. The longer I sat there lost in my thoughts, the more memories cascaded into my mind bringing more tears with each one. The burial was over more quickly than the funeral! I couldn't fathom the thought of staring at their caskets any longer!

Finally, the message came to an end. I was completely drained. I stood up and walked over to the caskets. I laid a hand on Kris's casket and said my final *Goodbye*. I heard the whistle of a train in the distance. I felt as if the sound was Kris saying *Goodbye, and I love you*. Warmth flooded my heart. God's heart was breaking too over my loss. I was so grateful He orchestrated a train whistle at just the right moment. Then I stepped over to Adam's casket with a superhero spray complete with red, yellow and blue flowers and even a ribbon which read, Mama's Superhero. I leaned over in a soft whisper and said, *Goodbye, Spiderman, mama loves you and misses you!* I turned and walked outside the tent and said goodbyes as quickly as possible to my family and friends. One person I wanted to make sure I hugged was Stefanie, the owner of the company I worked for. I wanted her to know how thankful I was for all her family was doing for me. I got back in the car to leave. All I wanted was to be with Conner! Finally in the car, I was exhausted and couldn't handle any more memories. I leaned my head on my sister's shoulder, wrapped up in Kris's shirt, and went to sleep. I slept almost the rest of the way back to Dallas.

Back at The Hospital

We finally got back to the hospital late in the evening. As we walked into Conner's room, the nurse told me Conner's neurosurgeon Dr. Wellington wanted to be called as soon as we got back. He wanted to talk in person. He was supposed to do Conner's spinal fusion the next day to stabilize his neck, where he was injured. The spinal fusion was going to be a very long and potentially life-threatening surgery. Why did he want to talk to me? My mind was not in the mood to speak with anyone!

Dr. Wellington walked into the room. He told me they had done another MRI, and Conner had crashed several times. Conner wasn't stable enough to go through the spinal fusion surgery the next day. Dr. Wellington then said the MRI showed what looked like global brain damage, which meant he had no brain activity. I asked him why that didn't show up before? As many scans as they had done the past several days, the diagnosis didn't make sense to me. He told me the only other possibility was an infection, and they were confident an infection was not the case.

He then told me I needed to think about Conner's future. I was done! I lost it! I told him we were done talking. Conner's life was in God's hands, not his! I got up to walk out of the room. As I was leaving, Dr. Wellington raised his voice. He told me I needed to sit down and discuss the matter like an adult. My parents looked at him and reminded him I had just buried my family, and he needed to have some respect! I ran out of the room and hid in the bathroom until I knew the doctor was gone! I asked God, *Why does it feel like I am getting punched in the face every time I turn around*?

After the doctor left, I asked the nurse if there was any way I could lay beside Conner for just a bit. He had so many tubes and wires coming from all directions. I thought the request would be impossible to accomplish. With the help of the Respiratory therapist, she was able to make this happen.

At the end of that traumatic Tuesday, enduring the funeral of my husband and oldest son, there was nothing better than cuddling up next to Conner. I would have loved to see his big blue eyes open up and say *mama*, but for that moment, I was content being able to lay next to him. I knew my God was bigger than any situation. God was my hope in tragedy. All I knew was I had to keep believing God had bigger plans than what was before my eyes. *Faith is confidence in what we hope for and assurance about what we do not see. Hebrews 11:1*

CONNER

The Family Meeting

The morning was dawning again over the Dallas Skyline, and in different circumstances, I might have enjoyed the view. Today, however, my baby boy was still in critical condition. Yesterday, the ICU doctors had asked for a meeting with me and close family members. I agreed to it, though, my last encounter with Dr. Dogwa was not positive. I knew they would tell me what I didn't want to hear. I wanted to hear hope in their voices. I wanted to know they were doing everything they possibly could to heal him. I wondered if they had given up on Conner and they were no longer trying as hard as they could to help him. Maybe that is why they called us together. I dreaded meeting with Dr. Dogwa. Thinking of the meeting made my stomach tie in knots. I felt my hands start to sweat, and I knew my pulse was up. I had already lost everything. How could they expect me to quit fighting for Conner? I knew meeting with them would not be a good experience! I had never met doctors so full of doom and gloom. I didn't sleep much the night before, not that I had gotten much sleep over the last week anyway. I kept praying over Conner, asking God to *please heal him completely and give me the strength to endure this meeting.*

The nurses changed shifts, and in walked our nurse, Christine. We had become close to her, and she was starting her twelve-hour shift with Conner. Conner had been her only patient because he was so critical. She spent her twelve-hour shifts in the room with us. She asked if we wanted to do the family meeting in Conner's room. I replied, *No.* I didn't want any negativity around him. We tried hard not to speak negatively about his condition in his presence. We wanted Conner to keep fighting. We tried to infuse as much positivity and joy in the room as possible. Even in an induced state coma, every time he heard my voice, his heart rate would go up. Christine went to find another place to hold the meeting. After several minutes, she came back and told us the ICU room next door was empty. They had moved some chairs in there for all of our family.

As we walk into the sterile, cold, empty ICU room, I quickly picked a chair and prayed
the meeting would be over quickly! My family and Kris's family all waited for Dr. Dogwa, the same doctor who could have been nicknamed Dr. Gloom. I already knew what he was going to advise.

Dr. Dogwa finally walks into the room. He was a tall and thin man. He also had a full black beard. He had arrogance radiating off of him like the heat from the sun. He pulled a stool up in front of me. He started talking with his accented voice, my mind wanted to tune him out. I did not want to listen to a person with no faith in my son's healing. I sat there and told myself to focus on what he was speaking to me.

As I focused in, he started saying, *As you know, Conner has sustained some severe injuries. His prognosis isn't good. He has a spinal cord injury at C1, C2, and C3. This is where the head connects to the spine. He will be a quadriplegic and left paralyzed from the neck down. He will never be able to take one breath on his own. Over the next several months, his muscles will start to tighten up due to inactivity, which will cause all of his extremities to draw up. He will end up having chronic pneumonia, which will eventually claim his life.* He continued, *What we thought was global brain damage is actually spinal meningitis due to spinal fluid leaking. It will be a miracle if he can even survive through the spinal meningitis, much less all of his other injuries.* Dr. Dogwa continued his prepared speech, the same speech he had already shared with us during each visit. It was all I could do not to stand up and say, Do you not believe in miracles? Our God healed the lame and brought Lazarus back from the dead! As he continued to speak, I recounted every memory of God's power from the Bible I could remember. Every negative word Dr. Dogwa spoke, I replaced with one of those memories and said, *Yes, you're right, Conner's situation does look bad, but my God can do anything! He can heal Conner.* With all my being, I wanted this doctor to see how great and awesome our God is.

His voice was cold, with no compassion. Then I heard his words, *What you need to realize is that Conner will have no quality of life. You need to let him go. We can place him in your arms and let you rock him until he passes. We will keep him comfortable, so you don't watch him struggle to pass.*

I looked over at my parents with tears welling up in my eyes, wondering if this guy is for real? Did he really just say that to me? He wants me to rock my son to his death after I just lost my whole family?

With tears of anger and hurt, I screamed out at him, *There is NO way I am letting Conner go! I don't believe God saved Conner from the wreck for me to give up on him now.* The wreck was unsurvivable. It was a miracle that Conner was still here. I had been crying out to God the last several days to please let Conner live. So why would I end Conner's life now? He was all I had left! I wasn't about to give up on Conner or God!

I proceed and ask, *How can you predict Conner's future after just a few days? You told me his left arm that is broken would take four weeks to heal. This injury is definitely more severe than a broken arm, so how can you say after a few days this is how his future will be?*

He hastily stood up, got closer to me, and said, *If you were in my country, this wouldn't be your decision. The decision would be mine. I would choose to end his life!* He continues, *You are being selfish, and YOU need to think about Conner's quality of life!* I responded, *This is my decision. My decision is to go on with Conner's life!*

When he stormed out of the room, all that was going through my head was, how could he be so cruel and cold to me, knowing everything I have lost and been through. Tears were streaming down my face. I couldn't understand why he was so worried about what life would be like for us. He wasn't going home with us to take care of Conner. Why did my decision bother him so much, choosing to go on with Conner's life?

Doctors are schooled to give you the worst-case scenario. They don't want to fill us with false hope, only to go home, and more medical problems arise. We wouldn't be prepared for them and would come back asking why they didn't explain what was medically happening. I didn't understand the no compassion or supporting my decision to go on with his life.

I sat there sobbing, and for the first time, I screamed out in anger at Kris! *What were you doing? How did you not see the dump truck? You have ruined our lives.* I felt like I couldn't breathe. The pain I was feeling was unbearable. At that moment, I claimed the Bible verse that says, *God is the same, yesterday, today, and forever. (Hebrews 13:8).*

I finally calmed down enough to leave the room that felt tainted to me. I knew in my heart Kris would never do anything to harm our boys. I felt so frustrated this had happened to Conner. I was utterly helpless. Our only hope was a miracle. I knew Kris loved our boys just as much as I did. I knew what happened was just a horribly tragic accident, and I would never have the answers as to how or why it happened.

I told my family I needed a moment to compose myself. I decided to go to the ICU waiting room to update my family and friends. Erin was waiting for my call. She kept my co-workers informed.

Opening the door to the waiting room, I see our family friend, Billie, standing there. I told him I needed to call Erin and asked him to listen in while I told her the diagnosis of Conner's condition. I didn't want to have to repeat this horrible story again today. I told Billie and Erin how *I wished God would give me a sign letting me know I made the right decision.* No sooner had those words came out of my mouth, the most beautiful rainbow I had ever seen appeared over downtown Dallas. I looked over at Billie and asked him, *Am I imaging this?* He responded, *It is real Sonya. I believe this is just another confirmation from God that you are doing the right thing.*

I told Erin I had to go, I needed to get back to Conner's room and tell my family about the rainbow. I ran back to Conner's room. The staff, visitors, nurses and doctors I ran past looked at me like something must have gone wrong. I ran inside the room. My mom and the nurse were looking out the window at the rainbow. I started crying as I explained I had just asked God for a confirmation, and immediately a rainbow appeared. They both gasped in shock and starting rejoicing with me! One of the scriptures I came across after the accident was one of the many I claimed repeatedly. Isaiah 40:31– *But those who hope in the Lord will renew their strength. They will soar on wings like eagles, they will run and not grow weary, they will walk and not faint.* To me, this Bible verse means God will give us strength when we are weak from facing a difficult challenge in our life. We also have to be patient in his timing! I wanted God to reach down and raise Conner up out of the bed immediately, but that wasn't God's plan, and he kept telling me to be patient.

Thirty-one Days in ICU
Tomorrow Doesn't Exist

It's incredible how time stands still inside a hospital room. I looked outside and saw the cars traveling up and down the interstate. I knew they were living a normal life unaffected by my own personal tragedy. They had no way of knowing what I was going through in my little corner of the world, but still, I envied them. They were able to go home to their families. They were able to celebrate special occasions and participate in sports. I sighed and moved away from the window. I knew I couldn't let my mind dwell there much longer. Despite my heartache and the machines beeping behind me, I had a peace about my decisions. I guess this is what the verse Philippians 4:7 means, *And the peace of God, which transcends all understanding, will guard your hearts and your minds in Christ Jesus.* The peace I felt that night didn't make sense based on my meeting with Dr. Dogwa. Knowing so many people were praying for Conner all over the world and the rainbow I saw outside the window, I knew God was with Conner and me. I just had to fix my mind on God.

The next morning after our family meeting, the Nurse Practitioner walked into our room. She told me she had nightmares all through the night about my decision to go on with Conner's life. She said, *Sonya, you don't understand what your life will be like when you take Conner home.* She continued, *I have a special needs child, and you don't understand the responsibility you're taking on.* I was furious! First of all, how dare she come in to say these things to me? In reality, my decision was none of her business! Second, why was she voicing her negative opinion in the room with Conner? I'm sure he heard everything. Even though he was in an induced coma, I knew he heard everything going on around him. I thought how heartless of her to come into his room and say those things. I left the room before she could say anything else or before I did something I would regret. I locked myself in the bathroom down the hall. It was the only place I could go to be alone. I stood over the sink and cried my heart out to God. I thanked

Him for the peace He gave me last night. I told Him I didn't think I could take any more negative people. I begged Him to give me strength. I marched to the desk and insisted on having a new Nurse Practitioner assigned to Conner's case.

As I left the desk, I whispered a prayer, *God, please don't let her still be in Conner's room when I return!* When I got back to the room, my mom was sitting in the rocking chair, just as upset as I was. I asked mom, *how could she be so heartless? They knew I had just buried my husband and son. Why wouldn't they think I would do everything I could to give Conner a chance?*

Later in the afternoon, our Pastor, Dr. Fannin, came to visit. I poured my heart out to him. I couldn't believe they would make such statements to me, especially around Conner. They were so negative. I felt like they lacked faith in God. I thought they were supposed to support the decisions I made. He asked me, *Sonya, can you make it through today?* I said, *Yes.* He responded with, *that is all you have to do. Just make it through today. Tomorrow doesn't exist, only today exists. Don't look into the future, it isn't there. All it will do is cause you fear. We aren't supposed to have a spirit of fear. Focus on today only. Where there is life, choose life!*

Our days seemed to be sprinkled with negativity and unbelief in God through our ICU doctors. If it wouldn't have been for our nurses supporting my decision, it would have made our time in ICU even more unbearable. For every negative remark, God sent positive reminders He was with us. We needed those! Even though I knew we were making the right decisions, others' negativity weighed heavily on us. A few days after Dr. Fannin had come by to see us, God sent another reminder we were not walking this journey alone. He wanted us to know He was with us. Kris had attended his fourth session for a class at our church called Letter's from Dad. As I mentioned earlier in the book, Kris's dad had abandoned his family when he was a little boy. He desperately wanted to be a good dad for his boys. In the course of the study, it helps dads learn how to write letters of blessings to their spouse, mom and children. A church in Dallas was also doing the same class. A man from our church had contacted them and advised that our family needed prayer. The church sent some people from their group and prayed over Conner. These two gentlemen become mighty prayer warriors for us. One of the gentlemen even had a son named Conner. One evening they asked our ICU nurse to bring their guitar and have a worship service for Conner. The nurse agreed as long as they didn't get too loud. That evening we had a worship and prayer service in Conner's ICU room. I was amazed! I felt the presence of God in his room, even after the praise and worship ended.

Conner's room quickly became the place where many nurses wanted to be assigned for their shift. We had hope in our great big God, and our hope was a light in a place filled with sadness. The joy we displayed through our deep sorrow was something few could understand. To some, our family was a mystery. The difference was we were not grieving as those who had no hope *(1 Thessalonians 4:13)*.

Until Conner could have the spinal fusion surgery to stabilize his neck, he would always need three nurses to move him. They had to be extremely careful when moving him because of his injuries. One wrong move could break his neck and kill him. There had to be a nurse at Conner's head and one on each side of him. Every time we watched him get moved, we held our breath in sheer panic and prayed.

Sometimes the presence and spirit of God can be a bit much for some people. Karen, the nurse at Conner's head, started getting antsy. She kept saying to the other nurse's something powerful was in the room, and she needed to leave. Karen begged to hurry up because the hair was standing up on her neck. As they got Conner repositioned, she went out to the nurse's station looking into Conner's room and just kept saying she could feel the spirit of God in the room. She had never experienced anything like it before. We prayed earlier in the evening for God to surround Conner with his mightiest guardian angels. After her experience, Karen was drawn to our room. She always worked the night shift. We would see her standing at the nursing station looking into our room. She later said, *Sonya, God has Conner in his hands, keep pushing forward.* More confirmation that we were making the right decision to choose life for Conner.

The outpouring of support from everyone blessed us. Family and Friends continued to visit us often throughout the week and weekend. We were so grateful to see everyone! We had great encouragement with everyone still supporting and loving us!

Around three weeks after the accident, the day came to do the spinal fusion surgery. The spinal Fusion was going to be a very long and life-threatening surgery. It entailed going in and fusing his neck at the place of the injury. They had to take a piece of his left rib to make a cast around his spine, then place rods on each side of the spine and screwed them into his skull. Despite the daily conversations with the medical team trying to talk me out of doing anything to prolong Conner's life, I kept reminding myself of my new latest phrase, Faith over Fear. One of my favorite scriptures is Hebrews 13:6, *Let your faith be bigger than your fear.*

A part of me was ready, and yet another part of me was beyond terrified. I felt like I was going step by step down a long hallway where I didn't know where the end was. I had to keep moving forward with God's strength. The medical team had informed me the spinal fusion would allow the C-collar to be taken off. The collar needed to come off because the pressure was creating sores on the side and back of his neck. The nurses constantly had to care for the wounds. I knew this also meant I would be able to hold my sweet boy again. I was beyond ready!

The thought of knowing Conner could die during surgery was terrifying. Dr. Wellington, our neurosurgeon, explained that getting him onto his stomach to do the surgery would be very tricky. It would take a lot of time to accomplish. If they moved him even an inch wrong, they would break his neck, which would ultimately kill him. If Conner crashed during the surgery, they would not be able to flip him over to revive him because they would break his neck. I was terrified for this surgery.

The whole time he was in surgery, I was a nervous wreck. I prayed for guardian angels to be in the operating room to protect Conner. The devil's mission is to kill, steal, and destroy. He definitely would want to stop anything that would make God's name great! At one point, I went and crawled up in my mom's lap, longing to be comforted for a moment. Watching the time tick by was enough to drive me insane! I felt like the clock was moving in extreme slow motion. I wanted this surgery to be over and successful!

Finally, after six long hours, our neurosurgeon walked into the ICU waiting room. We all held our breath waiting to hear the news. He led us out into the hallway. Myself, my family, and one of our friends, Shane, a physical therapist, walked out into the hallway. We were all trying to gauge the look on his face. Did we see hope in his eyes? His face was hard to read, and I didn't see the hope I longed for in his eyes. My heart started racing, afraid of what he was about to tell us.

He shared, *this was the worst spinal cord injury I've ever seen. I was able to get his neck stabilized, but he'll be paralyzed from the neck down with no hope of recovery.* I felt like he just punched me in the stomach! I blinked back tears. I was hoping to hold them off until he had left, but before I knew it, they were slowly making their way down my face. This was not the news I wanted to hear! He began to give me a long list of medical issues that would be wrong with Conner due to this high level of injury. I stopped him and said, *Right now, I do not want to hear all of this. Today was a stressful day for me, and all I need to know today is that the procedure was successful. The rest doesn't matter! I cannot hear any more negative news!* I just want to focus on today. He survived the surgery, which was a miracle in itself. My mind echoed silently, *faith over fear.*

I asked him if I could see Conner. He told me they were getting him situated in his room and would let me know when he was ready. After about fifteen minutes, I walked into his ICU room. My heart was breaking as I looked at him lying there in the hospital bed. I was thinking about how he said my little boy would never walk again. He said he would never be able to use his extremities. He said he would be on a ventilator for the rest of his life! This was my rambunctious little boy who was walking at eight months old and into everything. About a month before the accident, we had gone to the Zoo as a family. All he wanted was to get out of the wagon and walk. I knew if I had let him out, he would run off because he loved to run away from me. I wished today I could chase him once again. I caressed his sweet cheek. I began to touch each arm and leg and prayed over each one. I prayed Conner would not be completely paralyzed, and God would prove them wrong. I asked God again, *How could this be happening?*

I kept praying for a miracle! God was the only hope I had to cling to at that point. I knew no matter what Conner's condition was, I was still taking him home. I was determined I was going to give him the best life possible. I knew I needed him to survive for me to survive.

Hold My Boy Again

I finally got to hold my little boy in my arms. Since the accident, I had longed for this day. The nurse brought in a rocking chair for me to sit in. The ventilator, IV's and tubes Conner was hooked up and made this problematic. It took several nurses to make this happen. The nurse propped pillows up all around the chair's arms, which made it softer and more comfortable for Conner. As she laid him in my arms, my heart melted. Conner was starting to open his eyes occasionally. He still wasn't able to focus on me. I was finally able to hold my little boy and let him feel my love through holding him. I wanted so badly to hear him say, *mama*! I sat there for almost two hours rocking, loving and talking to him. It was the best two hours I had experienced since the wreck. I kept telling him I loved him and was so proud of him for continuing to fight hard. Kris was a huge Superman fan. I told Conner his daddy didn't realize he had a true superman as a son.

Every morning, the ICU doctor came into our room to give the respiratory therapist instructions on what to do for the ventilator. Then he would look over at me and back at the therapist and say, *the rest is just maintenance because mom won't accept it!* His words were gut-wrenching. Every day, they tried to convince me I had made the wrong decision. He tried so hard to get me to sign a Do Not Resuscitate (DNR) order. My answer was always the same, *No!* I couldn't understand why he kept torturing me! I looked forward to the days he was off, which weren't very many. I constantly reminded myself of the conversation with my pastor, *just make it through today, where there is life, choose life!*

Rest and Grieving

Exhaustion became a normal way of life for me. I had never understood the toll a hospital takes on a patient's loved ones until I experienced this with Conner. Between the stress of watching Conner continue to fight for his life and the constant negativity, life seemed difficult. We were surrounded by such sadness. So many families in the ICU area were dealing with dire situations. I was thankful for the large window we had, which let in lots of sunlight.

Staying in hotels became too expensive, even with the discount we received through the hospital. We were thankful when the Ronald McDonald House (RMH) had an opening. They only gave us one room, so we all took turns. Leaving Conner was difficult. Most days, I only went to the RMH room to get away for a few hours and take a shower. Erin started staying at the hospital with me on Saturday nights so my parents could take a break. I always needed someone with me. I didn't want to be alone in the hospital at night! When things got quiet at night, my mind had time to ponder all I had lost and all I was going through. I grieved over those losses some nights until my pillow couldn't hold any more tears. I tried to sob as quietly as possible. I didn't want Conner to hear me crying.

I believe God knew grieving Kris and Adam at the same time would be too much. I grieved in spurts, and I grieved for each of them separately. God has his way of protecting us. I had to focus on Conner and keeping him alive. If I had let my grief overcome me, it would have sent me into a downward spiral. I could have easily ended up in a very dark place. God knew Conner was going to be my saving grace.

I looked forward to the times my sister could be with us. That gave us all time to go and rest a bit. One of her favorite things was reading the book she bought him, *The Hiccupotumus, by Aaron Zenz* with various voices reenacting the different scenes. We wanted Conner to hear laughter and joy so that he wouldn't be scared. We wanted Conner to hear only positive things. Mustering up joy with the reality of our situation wasn't easy. There were still many tears being shed, but our focus was to do all we could to give Conner hope to keep fighting. The Bible says, *"A joyful heart is good medicine, but a crushed spirit dries up the bones"* Proverbs 17:22. Our God promised us in His word, He could move mountains (Matthew 17:20), so with all that was in us, we clung to His promises. We were all trying to keep Conner's spirits up.

Looking back, I know God gave us those moments to sustain our faith as we continued to fight the negativity surrounding us. A Neurologist and his assistant came into the room to check Conner's brain activity. The room had to be dark and quiet as he hooked electrodes up to Conner's head. The doctor wanted to watch his brain waves activity and do a hearing test. The ICU doctors had assumed the spinal meningitis was due to the leaking of spinal fluid. They thought it had caused global brain damage. After the Neurologist finished the test, he told me there was no brain activity, and Conner had global brain damage. Conner would be blind, deaf, and have no emotions. He went on to say Conner would be a vegetable for the rest of his life. I was devastated by listening to the Neurologist. I struggled to believe him. For days when Conner heard my voice, his heart rate would go up. I couldn't believe what the Neurologist was saying. The ICU doctors were giving him heavy sedatives to keep him in a coma state. I wondered how the test could have been accurate. The doctor's logic made no sense to me. That was a restless night. I was up and down most of the night checking on Conner. I struggled with everything going on.

Katrina stayed with me at the hospital that night after the test. The next morning mom came back to the hospital. She talked me into going to the RMH so I could rest for a bit. I was still restless. I read my Bible and asked God to please show me that somehow this test was incorrect. Mom later called me and said, *Conner had a surprise for me when I got back.* I thought, what surprise can that be since he's not even responding right now.

After we hung up, I couldn't help but rush back to the hospital, wanting to know the surprise. As I walked into the ICU room, I walk up to Conner's bed with mom and my sister standing on either side. My mom leaned down and asked Conner if he can move his hand for her. He immediately picks up his right hand. She asked him to raise his hand again, and he did. He kept doing this several times on command. Mom told me that she and Katrina had been praying and reading healing scriptures over Conner. I cried and praised God! He had answered another prayer. I was thankful. He gave me another sign to keep pushing forward in faith. He has a plan for us. One of my favorite verses is Jeremiah 29:11 *For I know the plans I have for you, declares the Lord, plans to prosper you and not to harm you, plans to give you a future and a hope.* God had saved Conner from the accident. No matter what the doctors said about Conner, only what God wanted to do through Conner's life mattered. The doctors had said Conner wouldn't be able to move from the neck down. They were wrong! They said he couldn't hear us, they were wrong! God provided the hope we needed to keep moving ahead. We all rejoiced in what God had shown us!

We told the nurse about Conner. She watched him follow through with the command. She brought the doctor in, and of course, Conner wouldn't move his hand. The doctor said his response was merely reflexes. I was extremely frustrated. We knew better. His movement was not reflexes. He was moving on command when we asked him. Why was it so difficult for them to believe in the miraculous? Maybe God wasn't ready for the doctors to see what Conner could do. I wanted the doctors to see they were wrong about Conner. I wanted to show them my baby still had life in his body! Through my experience, I had learned that life wasn't about my timing. Everything is all in God's timing.

Prayer Warriors

God placed amazing people in our lives during our time in ICU. The Heights Church in Richardson was one of the first churches to embrace us. The pastor at the church found out about our accident through Katrina. Their prayer team prayed fervently for us. I looked forward to all of the prayer grams that were sent during these trying times. (I still receive these prayer grams even now fourteen years later from The Heights Church. One of the heights ministers Dave Lyons has continued to follow Conner's progress.) Prayer grams from several churches reminded us of how much God loved us.

Turning Point Church, another church in the Dallas area, also adopted us within a couple of weeks after the accident. We are still not sure how they knew about our family. God always knows what we need and has a way of connecting people. He knew we needed a church family to surround us since we were far away from our own church home. The pastor had a daughter the same age as Conner. Our story tugged at his heart. Church members came and sat with Conner some Sunday mornings so we could attend their church service. On the Sundays we attended, they always said a special prayer for us. They would have me sit down in a chair and surround me to pray over me. I felt the presence of God during those prayers. Feelings of peace, gratitude and joy surrounded me. The comfort I felt in those moments was indescribable. I was thankful I was sitting down during these prayer times, or my legs probably would have gone out from under me. Those prayer times were powerful!!

One day at the hospital, mom and Choc got on the elevator and were very upset. We had just received more negative news. Just as the door was fixing to close, a couple walked up and got onto the same elevator. Noticing that Mom and Choc were upset, the gentlemen asked if they were okay. Choc told them our story. The couple's hearts broke for us. The couple asked if they could pray with them. The man prayed a powerful prayer over them. After the prayer, the woman asked if they could pray over Conner. Choc shared Conner's room number with the couple and told them they were more than welcome to pray over Conner. He figured, the more people who prayed for Conner, the better.

Our new prayer friends told mom and Choc that God had placed them in the hospital for such a time as this! Their one-month-old baby girl was in an ICU room down the hall from us, battling Leukemia. Mom told me their story and how they wanted to come pray for Conner. I thought, how amazing! Their daughter was in ICU fighting for her life, and they believed the whole purpose of their battle was to be there to pray for Conner. The couple was outstanding and unselfish! They came to our room and faithfully prayed for Conner every day, and not just little prayers. We had church in our room. We returned the favor and prayed with them for their baby girl. A few weeks later, they reached out to us to let us know she was cancer-free and she was being released from the hospital! We serve an incredible God who knows our needs before we ask and will put the right people in our path when we are struggling. In those moments, we have to recognize them as the activity of God in our lives.

We were finally nearing the end of our ICU stay. The doctors had decided we could be transferred down to the pulmonology floor. We were introduced to our new Pulmonologist doctors. These two doctors ended up being a blessing in our lives. Instead of constant doom and gloom every day from the ICU doctors, we had doctors who supported our decision to go forward with Conner's life. They even had a plan for us to get home. The first step was moving to the pulmonology floor for a few more weeks to give Conner more time to heal. When Conners body was well enough, they would move us to another facility in Dallas. At the new facility they would train us how to take care of Conner. We would have to go through Respiratory Therapy school for six weeks.

One afternoon while I was alone in the ICU room rocking Conner, Dr. Longhorn, one of our Pulmonologist, walked in. He told me there were issues with our insurance, not covering the other facility. He told me no matter what, even if he had to eat the cost, Conner would be going. I looked at him with tears in my eyes, thanking him! I told him I was happy to have a doctor with compassion. He told me that sometimes people need to do good things for good people. He felt like this was one of those situations. We wouldn't have been able to go home with Conner if we couldn't get to this facility for training. As he walked out of the room, I thanked God for this blessing. God always comes through.

Not even five minutes after our Pulmonologist walked out, in came Dr. Smith, the "nice" ICU doctor. The two ICU doctors were like good-cop and bad-cop. Dr. Smith didn't agree with my decision either to go on with Conner's life. I truly believe he came into the room because I was holding Conner and couldn't go anywhere. Dr. Smith pulled up a stool beside me and started telling me he needed to talk to me about what Conner's future would look like. I was getting mad! They knew we did not like them talking negative things over Conner. He had already proved to me he didn't care about what I thought was best for Conner. Dr. Smith said Conner would have chronic pneumonia. The pneumonia would eventually claim his life. He said we probably were only extending his life by a year. Dr. Smith advised that due to lack of using his muscles, they will all start tightening and drawing up, and his extremities would make him look like a pretzel.

I couldn't believe what he implied next! Dr. Smith said, *Sonya, it's your choice to end Conner's life, not your parents*! I guess he assumed they were making me go on with Conner's life. He had no idea who I was, the strength I had, and that I was a strong-willed mother who would have done anything for her child to survive. I told him, *This is not my parents leading the way. Ask them if they can change my mind on anything I am passionate about!* I looked him straight in the eyes and said, *You cannot predict Conner's future. I am sick and tired of you all trying to push me to end his life. This is my decision to go on with Conner's life, not my parents. It's not up for discussion any longer!* We were just a few days away from getting out of ICU, and they were still pushing me to end Conner's life.

Just as we were getting ready to get out of ICU, Conner's left lung collapsed. I was scared because he was struggling to breathe. They called in Dr. Silver, our other Pulmonologist. Dr. Silver had to do a surgical procedure called a bronchoscopy. He went down through the trach with a camera to see if anything was restricting his airways. He came out to give us the findings. The first words out of his mouth where *I don't know what these ICU doctors are telling you, but they told me I didn't need to sedate Conner because he has no feeling. They said he was in a vegetable state.* He then said *I promise you that little boy is not in a vegetable state and felt what I did to him."* His exact words were, *Conner was pissed off that I was messing with him.* This was another affirmation from God. He told us he had a lot of mucus plugs in his airways, which caused the collapsed lung. He cleaned all of them out and would get aggressive with his breathing treatment plan to pop the lung back open. Not that I wanted Conner's lung to collapse by any means, but I was thankful for the affirmation Conner was very aware of what he was doing and showed emotion about it.

We spent a total of thirty-one days in ICU before moving down to the Pulmonary Floor. I was never more excited than to be moving off the ICU floor. We were sad to leave our nurses but happy to get away from all the negative doctors. We were one step closer to going home. We experienced lots of heartaches over the course of the thirty-one days, and yet, we also saw the power of God move tremendously in our lives. Every time we were knocked down with devasting news, God immediately put someone in our path to give us the affirmation we needed and show us He was in control.

Moving to Pulmonary Floor

What an exciting day to finally be moving out of ICU! Conner still had a huge uphill battle to fight, but we were now with doctors who truly cared for Conner. They had caring hearts and wanted to help us get back home. Even though I didn't know what home would look like for us, I couldn't dwell there. I would soon have to figure out a new normal for Conner and me. I wasn't ready to deal with what things would be like at home in the upcoming months. I focused on what was happening at the moment. We were looking forward to having a little more privacy and our own bathroom with a shower. No more community bathrooms and showers. There is nothing worse than getting into the shower and someone knocking on the door even though the sign shows occupied. They want you to hurry so they can take a shower as well.

Things were a little different. We didn't have a nurse with us all the time. On this floor, the nurses had three to four kids they took care of on their shift. The nurses almost immediately started putting Conner prone on his stomach for an hour daily. This helps the secretions not settle in his lungs and cause pneumonia. The first time they did this, I couldn't figure out how in the world they could do this with him on a ventilator. They were lots of ventilator kids on this floor. They had a lot of experience at placing their vent patients in this position. Conner didn't like the transition over to his stomach initially, but immediately after he was positioned, he seemed very content. It probably felt good getting all the pressure off of his back and rear. We gave him a good back massage every time they put him on his stomach.

The nurses slowly started teaching us how to take care of Conner, so we would know how to do some things before moving to the other facility. They taught us the nursing side of things. Never in my life did I think I would be learning how to hook a food pump up for my child or learn how to care for him on a ventilator. I began to learn a lot about the settings on the ventilator and what they meant.

I will never forget how scared we were to take the ventilator off him for even one second. I wasn't sure how we were going to dress him. We would have to take the ventilator off to put a shirt over his head. One day while dad and Donna were there, mom and I went to the closest mall and bought all button-up shirts for Conner. I was determined not to take the ventilator off of him. What is funny is the respiratory therapist explained to us that taking the vent off for a few seconds is no different than us going underwater and holding our breath. I still didn't care. I wasn't comfortable taking him off yet. At the moment, button-up shirts were the best option for me.

A few days later, I needed to change his trach out for the first time. The thought of changing his trach was scary. I didn't want to hurt Conner in any way. They had done a tracheotomy where they made an incision on the neck's anterior aspect and opened a direct airway through an incision in the trachea. Then they place a tracheostomy (trach) tube into the hole to keep it open for breathing.

Our Respiratory Therapist (RT), Jordan, came into the room and asked me if I was ready to do my first trach change. I told him *no, not really*! I was terrified, but I knew I had to learn to change the trach. We had to change his trach once a week so that we could clean it. We didn't want bacteria setting up and causing an infection.

I am so thankful that Jordan was patient with me. He told me he would pull the trach out for me, and all I had to do was put in the new one. I looked at Conner and told him I was sorry if I hurt him, which was my biggest fear. Taking Conner's trach out was all new to us. RTs did this all the time. I had no clue what this even felt like for Conner or if changing the trach hurt. I didn't want to be the one to hurt him. Every time he would ask me if I was ready, I would say yes and then quickly start telling him no as soon as he was about to pull the trach out. This went on for what seemed like an eternity, but probably only about fifteen minutes. Finally, he said we are going to do this together. As he pulled the trach out, he guided my hand to place the new trach. It wasn't hard to do, but I was thinking to myself, am I ever going to be able to change the trach? How am I going to get over my fear of this? All I knew to do was ask God to give me the courage to accomplish this task. Now changing the trach isn't a big deal to me.

My sister and I went home to pick out the headstones for Kris and Adam. I was not looking forward to it. I was glad Katrina could go with me. Driving back, she began to share some of the research she had been doing on spinal cord injuries. Katrina said she had discovered a place in Baltimore, Maryland. It is called the Kennedy Krieger Institute. They specialize in spinal cord injuries and work with pediatrics. She had read stories about their facility, sharing how spinal cord injury patients were retraining their nerve endings to make new pathways. They were able to move again in ways they were told they wouldn't. In particular, one person had completely healed his spinal cord injury through therapy and was now able to walk again. I was amazed! When I asked her the cost, I couldn't imagine how we would ever go. Katrina said she believed God would make a way when the time was right.

We pulled up to the business with the headstones and walked in to talk with the owners. I wanted to do something extraordinary with the headstone to make it more personal. I wanted to include a letter in my handwriting on the backside of both Kris and Adam's headstone. I wanted to share with others what a great husband and dad Kris was to the boys and me. I wanted everyone to know how imaginative Adam was and how much he loved Spiderman. I was so grateful they were able to accommodate my requests.

We kept our trip short to Ardmore. I ran by the house to pick up a few things for myself. It was only my second trip home since the accident. Life still felt so strange, pulling up and not seeing Kris's truck. The house was so silent as we walked inside. All that was left of our family was memories. This is not how I planned for my summer to go this year. I ran my hand over Adam's Spiderman costume, still on the chair. I longed to turn around and see him running around as Spiderman. I had called him Spiderman a thousand times a day. If I could only have one more day with him. I picked up my things and went to my mom's house to get what she needed.

Over the summer, I had found out a few more details about the accident. The funeral home director suggested that because of Kris's injuries, he believed he threw his body in front of the boys at the last second to shield them from the impact of the accident. He sacrificed his life for them.

Once we arrived back at the hospital, we stayed with Conner and gave mom a break. She could go over to the Ronald McDonald House (RMH) to rest for a while and eat supper. One blessing of staying at the RMH are the groups that come every day to serve lunch and supper. They come bearing hot meals and sometimes gifts or entertainment for the families. The groups may not truly understand how much help their service provides for families impacted by tragedy and sickness. The meals help families financially.

On the pulmonology floor, Conner was being weaned off more and more every day from the medications they had him on. I loved seeing his big blue eyes when they popped open. I wondered what he was thinking. He was waking up to a new reality about his life, which was different from his memories. Before the accident, he had discovered how to climb up to Adam's top bunk, and we found him just as he jumped off from the top. Like many parents, I was scared to death. Because of this, we removed the ladder going up to the top bunk bed. My mind also drifted to the countless dance parties we often had in the living room. He loved to dance! What would he be able to do for entertainment now? Though my heart was heavy for Conner's losses and my own, I continued to remind myself that we just have to get through today. I once again fixed my mind on faith over fear.

On my drive back from the RMH one day, I came upon a movie theater. The boys would have been so excited to go see some of the animated movies over the summer. As I glanced at the movie posters, I saw the poster for Superman Returns. Kris and I had planned to see the movie on our next date night. Both Kris and Adam would have loved to have seen the Superman movie over the summer.

There were some days when I felt like I was living out the scene in a terrible movie. A movie about someone else's life. I wish so much I could turn back time and enjoy the last two weeks I had with my family one more time. I knew Kris and Adam were in God's presence and enjoying all I had ever heard about heaven. My heart still ached over how much I missed them. I was thankful I was going to lunch with some co-workers today. The owner, Stefanie, let half the ladies from the office come down once a week to take me to lunch and check on Conner. The other half came the opposite week. I always looked forward to my lunch dates with them. Shane, the Physical Therapist I transcribed for, had become very invested in Conner's life. Shane came down to the hospital, usually once a week. It was a blessing to have interactions with my office family.

During July, God continued to amaze us! We started noticing Conner moving his hand more and more. When we moved to the pulmonary floor, Shane even noticed Conner moving more and responding to our voices. Conners movements weren't just reflexes like the ICU doctors kept trying to say. His responses were very encouraging to us all. Shane told us some things to start doing with Conner. He was ready for us to get home so he could start working with him.

A few weeks after being on the Pulmonary floor, the time came to start the transition to the other facility. We were a little apprehensive about this next chapter and what all it would entail. We knew the move was the final step before going home. We were going to miss our nurses, whom we all grew to love! They became family to us. We had one night nurse on the pulmonary floor named Louisa. She spoiled Conner rotten. All the nurses spoiled him, but Conner was truly her favorite baby at the time. She would come in and tell me to lay down and go to sleep, and she would take care of Conner. Louisa would sit there and rub Conner's head for however long it took for him to fall asleep. She knew I wouldn't go to sleep if he was awake. She knew I needed rest. All the nurses on this floor were so much fun. We thanked God daily for blessing us with the best nurses through our time at the Kids Hospital in Dallas. The pulmonary floor was a happy environment. They would walk down the hall with their wireless speaker playing music and dancing in and out of the patient rooms trying to make a fun environment. It was such a contrast to the ICU floor. Some of those kids spent most of their life in and out of the hospital.

Since Conner's condition was progressively getting better, I was able to relax a little more. I had more downtime on this floor. Doctors and nurses were not constantly in and out like they were on the ICU floor. It was good and bad. With more downtime came more waves of grief. The impact of losing Kris and Adam was starting to set in even more. When going through grief, you never know when the emotions will hit. When it does hit, I learned I had to go through the process of the pain. It would be easy to try and push this pain aside and try your best not to deal with it. The reality is that eventually, you will deal with it. Pushing grief away won't work forever. It is hard to go through the pain of losing a loved one, and fourteen years later, I still have my days when I grieve my family. I believe the pain of losing a child and my husband will always be there.

I was going through a rollercoaster of emotions. I started finding that Christian music was great therapy for me. The more I listened to it, the more I became uplifted. I also started playing music for Conner. Christian music was uplifting and had a positive effect on both of us. The music was especially helpful on the days where I felt anxious about going back home for the first time. Somehow our God would help us make it through this time. I chose to focus on the verse Isaiah 41:10, *"Do not fear for I am with you do not be dismayed for I am your God. I will strengthen you and help you, I will uphold you with my mighty right hand." (NIV)* I prayed, *"Thank you, for this promise, God! I can't imagine going through all of this without you. Today, I will take hold of your mighty right hand, and we will do this together."*

The Rehab and Training Facility

Almost two months later, we finally headed over to The Rehab and Training facility. I was a little apprehensive. I was unsure sure of what to expect at this new facility, plus I wasn't thrilled to share a room with another child. The plan was to start Conner on therapy while mom, dad, Donna and I went through six weeks of Respiratory therapy school, then we would be able to go home. I longed for home, but I also knew going home wasn't going to be easy!

Mom followed behind us as I rode in the ambulance that transported Conner to The Rehab and Training Facility. When we arrived I started to panic. The building was older on the inside and needed an upgrade. The outside of the building was all brick. The Pulmonary floor at the hospital had been so full of life. All of the rooms had large windows looking out over the Dallas Skyline. Even though we endured some difficult days in the hospital, the sunshine pouring through those big open windows seemed to melt away some of the sadness and replace it with hope in the days ahead. I was blinking back the tears as they walked us to the room we were assigned. How were we going to spend the next six weeks in rehab? The facility was a totally different environment. I missed our family of nurses already!

When we walked into our room, I was stunned. The room was tiny, a ten by twelve area with one hospital bed for Conner and a baby crib for our roommate. How would all of us be able to spend time with Conner in this space? The other family would need room for their family as well. As my eyes scanned the room for where mom and I would sleep, my eyes fell on a tattered green chair in the corner. I sat down to see if the chair reclined. The recliner protested as I pushed the lever, but it finally gave way for the footrest to come up. The seat was so hard, I couldn't imagine sleeping on it. There was no space between this chair and Conner's bed as the room was so small. Tears streamed down my face as I tried to take in this new environment. I got up and laid some of Conner's belongings down on the floor. I was thankful the room was very clean, just very outdated with sailboat wallpaper on part of the wall.

I glanced over to the other child lying in the bed adjacent to Conner's. I was disappointed we didn't have a private room. We loved playing Christian music and making the room a happy place. We felt awkward to include another child knowing nothing of her situation or her parents. The facility felt more like a nursing home environment for kids, which I guess it was to some of the patients. For some of the kids, the facility was home because they didn't have anyone to care for them. Some parents had to work and couldn't find nursing staff for care in their homes. Other parents didn't feel comfortable taking their child home.

I tried to find something to be joyful about in our circumstance. I realized Conner had the side of the room with a window. Though not as big as the ones in our previous rooms, I was able to look out the window and open the blinds to let in the sunshine. A little baby girl was on a ventilator in the baby crib in the room with us. I watched as she kicked her legs and made cooing noises. My heart broke for her.

We had to start all over again. The pediatric and rehab doctors came in, did assessments and asked me a million questions. I was wondering why they asked me so many questions. They had all of his paperwork. I wanted them to be done. I struggled to fight back the tears. I could tell from their expressions, they didn't have any hope of Conner's quality of life improving. The responses I received from them showed me the rehab doctors were going off of what the doctors from the hospital had told them and strictly by textbook. If the doctors paid attention, according to the textbook, Conner shouldn't have been able to do the things he was doing. Any person of faith knows God is bigger than the medical books. The doctors believed Conner was paralyzed from the neck down with a significant brain injury. I wanted to scream, This is not true! We had seen signs of movement! He isn't what the ICU doctors said he would be. I also wanted to tell them, You don't know my God!

As soon as the doctors were gone, I looked at my mom and said, *I don't want to be here*. All kinds of emotions were sweeping over me. I knew we had to be there to learn how to take care of Conner, but I desperately wanted to pick Conner up and run away. I prayed for God to make our six weeks of training go fast.

We checked in on a Friday, which gave us the weekend to get into a new routine. Honestly, as scared as I was about going home, I just wanted my home. Our training started on the following Monday. My mom and I took turns staying every other night with Conner. Between the uncomfortable recliner, the medical staff in and out of our room and having a roommate, we didn't get much sleep. We found a local church that owned some apartments not far from the facility. The church rented the rooms to people who were in the Rehab facility for twenty dollars a night. It was a blessing for us financially, but I will spare you the details of the conditions. We wished that the Ronald McDonald House wasn't so far away from this facility.

Training Day

By the time Monday rolled around, I was ready to get our week started. Conner was also starting physical and occupational therapy. I was excited to see what they would be doing with him. Candice Lockhart, RRT, RCP was the Respiratory Educator Coordinator who did all of the ventilator training. As she introduced herself, I started getting nervous about what all this would entail. Mom, Dad, Donna and I went through the training. Choc hung out with Conner so he wouldn't be alone. I was the primary caregiver, with mom as secondary. Dad and Donna were our back-ups.

From the expressions on their faces, I could tell all of the medical staff were surprised by the family support for Conner and me. Several of the kids on ventilators wouldn't be going home, because there weren't two trained caregivers. I had both sets of my parents involved. Dad was juggling going back and forth with work. He and mom worked for a local tire plant in our town. Donna was retired from the tire plant, and Choc was a cattle rancher. The tire plant leadership was understanding and supportive through all of this. Before we could go home, I had to room in forty-eight hours. Mom had to room in for twenty-four hours. We had to do all of Conner's respiratory care without assistance. At the end of the six weeks, they would test us, making sure we knew exactly how to take care of Conner.

Candice explained our training and schedule and then took us to a lounge area across from our room for our first session. She placed a ventilator on the round table in front of us with a package of vent circuits. She asked me, *Can you put the circuit on the ventilator?* In my mind, I was thinking, Oh no, am I supposed to already know how to do this? They didn't teach us this at the hospital. My heart started racing like a kid in school who doesn't know the answer when the teacher calls on you. I responded, *No, I have no idea.* I expected her to be upset with me. She was the complete opposite of being upset, as she knew I wouldn't know how to put the ventilator together yet.

The training was unbelievable. Candice was a fantastic teacher. She was so patient and ended up becoming like family to us. Candice listened to us about the things we were seeing with Conner when doctors wouldn't listen. With Candice spending as much time with us as she did, she began to see what we had been explaining to the doctors.

A Breath of Fresh Air

One day, I needed to go home. Fundraiser accounts were being set up for us. These accounts required mine and my stepsister Tracy's signature. I am so thankful Tracy was able to take care of all of my bills and banking. She also helped with getting thank you cards out and mailed. Tracy was another blessing from God.

When I got back to Dallas later in the evening, mom told me she and Candice had taken Conner outside for a walk to get him some fresh air. It was a beautiful sunny day. The second they walked back inside, Conner pouted up and began to cry. Candice immediately said to my mom, *Manaw, he is completely aware of what is going on! Look, he doesn't want to go back into the building.* Her eyes were opened to the discrepancies between Conner's medical records and what she had just experienced being outside. We were so thankful she experienced what we had been telling everyone. Before the accident, getting Conner back inside was always a fight. This incident proved my little Conner was still in there fighting this battle in front of him. He was so strong.

Frustration

I was extremely disappointed in the physical and occupational therapy. The therapist believed what the prior doctors had told them. They thought Conner was paralyzed from the neck down, so the only therapy he needed was stretching of his extremities. I wanted the therapist to get Conner up and go to the gym to do more extensive therapy like they were doing with other kids.

We tried explaining we were seeing him move his arms and legs and responding to pain, but just like at the hospital, they felt his movement were "just" his reflexes. The textbook says if you have a spinal cord injury, there is no hope for recovery. I kept thinking there was some reason God did not want their eyes to be open to what we were seeing. When we feel surrounded by the negativity we see all around us, we need God to open our spiritual eyes to realize God is surrounding us. He will fight for us! (Exodus 14:14) When we see the battle, God sees the victory. Imagining God's angels filling up our room and surrounding Conner was the only way I could fight the negativity. I couldn't wait for the day they understood Conner had partial movement on command. Then they will know God is real. They will know that God does perform miracles.

Even though I knew God could move mountains, there were still days my mama heart struggled with the constant negativity. Dr. Sampson, our pediatric doctor at the rehab facility, was a good doctor. However, I started getting frustrated with him. He was not listening to anything we said about Conner's movements. One day Conner kept dropping his oxygen saturations. He looked as if he were bearing down like he was trying to have a bowel movement. We knew they were giving him food with extra iron, which could cause constipation. He hadn't had a good bowel movement in a couple of days. Mom asked Dr. Sampson about the added iron. His response was the spinal cord injury caused bowel issues. Which we knew spinal cord injuries do cause bowel issues, but at this moment we knew the issue was from the added iron. He didn't believe Conner's oxygen levels were dropping due to a bowel movement. In his opinion, Conner had no feeling or the ability to bear down to have a bowel movement on his own.

I asked him to spend some time in our room and watch. As we continued, our conversation got pretty heated. The argument got so heated between us that the nurse ended up covering up Conner's ears. I had lost my cool. I was tired of Dr. Sampson coming in our room for just a few seconds to do an assessment then argue with me about what we were seeing. The doctor thought I was just a mom who didn't want to accept her son's prognosis. However, in the end, he did agree to stop giving Conner the food with the extra iron. Guess what, Conner's bowels went back to normal after stopping the iron. We felt like we had to fight for Conner's health. We realized we had to become the experts on Conner to ensure he got everything he needed to continue to progress. Our Pulmonologists were the only ones who weren't negative all the time. It was a breath of fresh air when I saw them walk into the room.

Coming Around

A Neurologist named Emma came twice a week and did a coma scale on Conner. She explained that Conner's brain was slowly waking up, which took time for the brain to come out of a coma. Every week he kept dropping more and more on the coma scale. She was very pleased with his progress. Every week Conner started getting more and more alert and responding to us. He started getting his little Conner personality back, even though he wasn't able to respond verbally. It was hard for him to compensate talking over a ventilator, and since Conner was only saying a handful of words, understanding him was even more complicated. I remember seeing him cry with no sound. I longed to be able to hear his voice again. Even though I didn't want to see him cry, I did want to hear his sweet voice again.

I frequently played fun kid Christian music, lots of Veggie Tales CD's, for Conner to keep the situation as fun and upbeat as possible. One of mine and Conner's favorite songs was "Veggie Tales singing God of Wonders". We would listen to the song over and over. I am sure the medical staff was tired of hearing the music every time they came into our room, but the only thing that mattered was the song made Conner and myself happy.

My family did everything they could to keep Conner's spirits up. Dad would sing Conner silly songs and read books to Conner. Mom sang some of her favorite hymns and silly songs. Our roommate loved the music as well. We were determined as a family Conner would have an opportunity to be a little boy. We weren't going to let his circumstances define him. God continued to give us so many confirmations He was with us. We had to treat Conner as if God was healing his body despite what the doctors said about him. I continued to whisper in the moments fear gripped me, I am choosing *"faith over fear"*.

Leah, one of the respiratory therapists, started to notice Conner was over breathing the ventilator. He had started doing this back in the hospital. Leah told our pulmonologist Dr. Longhorn about Conner over breathing the ventilator. Dr. Longhorn gave orders to start turning down settings on his ventilator. We were so excited, something I was told he would never be able to do. After a few weeks, they turned his breath rate to zero. I was nervous. I wanted this badly. I longed for him to be able to breathe on his own. I was afraid he would not be able to. He went for thirty minutes with no issues. To say my family and I were ecstatic was an understatement. I had tears streaming down my face and was praising God. Over the next several days, the therapist kept adding more time. He got up to four hours and was doing great. I wanted to shout from the rooftops what an awesome God we serve! I knew God would keep showing up and giving us signs of life inside of Conner. No matter what the doctors believed, we were seeing the miracles unfold.

He was still actually on the ventilator, but they would turn his breath rate to zero breaths per minute instead of twenty breaths per minute. Conner still needed the pressure and peep support to keep his lungs open and compensate for breathing through all the tubing. Even though he was initiating taking his breaths, his lungs were still very weak. He couldn't take a big deep breath. Despite being told he would never initiate one breath on his own according to the ICU doctors. Conner was coming around none the less.

We had to put a hold on taking Conner to zero on the breath rate. Jan, a lady from the local church who had adopted us in, sat with Conner one Sunday morning so we could go to their church. It was the first time I had left Conner without a family member being there. When we returned to Conner's room, the doctors told us Conner had crashed, and they had the medical cart and was about to shock him. My heart sank. I kept having the same thoughts, I wasn't here, what if he would have died and I wasn't here? Would this have happened if I would have stayed? What caused the lapse? God, what did I do wrong? Did I make a bad decision to go to church? I was only gone for a couple of hours. How could this have happened? We were doing so well. He had to have been scared. I am sure he wanted his mama. I felt so horrible. I kept loving on him and telling him I was so sorry I wasn't there when he was hurting. The same time he was crashing, the church was saying a special prayer for Conner. A powerful prayer that gave me chill bumps. I genuinely believe in the power of prayer and believed having prayer during the moment Conner crashed was what had saved his life.

Conner's body still had a lot of healing left to do. Dr. Longhorn said, *Now we know we can take his breath rate to zero, let's not stress his body out any further until he is healed more and becomes stronger.* I was disappointed. I wanted to see him get off the ventilator so badly, but I also knew everything would be in God's timing. I didn't want to stress Conner's body out to the point he would crash on us again. No matter how bad I wanted to get him breathing on his own.

As Conner became more and more alert, we could tell he was getting tired of all the medical staff constantly doing assessments, breathing treatments and just everything being done to him. I brushed his teeth every morning with a mouth swab. One morning, I guess he did not want me in his mouth, and he bit down and broke the swab off the stick. I immediately panicked. I did not want him to swallow the swab. Mom ran and got the nurse. I got him to open his mouth a tiny bit, and she stuck her finger in to grab it and he clamped down hard on her finger. He had no intention of letting go of her finger. Luckily, she did have a hold of the swab, so he wasn't going to swallow it. We could tell she was in extreme pain, she had sweat rolling off of her forehead. The more we tried to get Conner to open his mouth, the harder he clinched down. You could see the fury in his eyes. He was probably so tired of being messed with, and his mouth was the only thing he had complete control over. After almost fifteen minutes, we finally got her finger free. I felt horrible. I kept apologizing to her. That incident made it easy to talk the staff into letting us switch to a regular toothbrush!

Ready to Go Home

The training was finally coming to an end. This meant I had to "room in" for my forty-eight hours. I would do this in two twenty-four-hour shifts. Mom only had to do one twenty-four hour shift. We had to do all of his breathing treatments during "room in" time. The treatments were every four hours around the clock. While doing his treatments, the respiratory therapist would watch us and check us off if we delivered his treatments correctly. Because he was on several different breathing treatment medicines, the treatment sessions took us around twenty to thirty minutes. We did not get much sleep. Once we had finished all of our "rooming in" and passed (which we did with flying colors), it was finally time to start the process of going home.

We had to get set up with a home health company to get private duty nursing. We had to have a direct medical company to get all of Conner's monthly medical supplies. All of this was very overwhelming to me. I kept thinking, I just want to go home and not have a bunch of strangers in my house all the time. I was apprehensive about having private duty nursing. I needed to go home and figure out how to have a new normal for Conner and me. I knew I had a lot to face. He would need twenty-four-hour care, seven days a week. I wanted time to process all I had been through these last few months by myself. I wanted to watch old family movies with Conner and curl up with things that reminded me of Kris and Adam.

The home health company made plans to have a hospital bed delivered to my house. They would have the bed set up before we returned home. I thought to myself, what do you mean they are going to go into my house and change Conner's room? I didn't know what to think or feel going through this whole process.

Dr. Sampson, the pediatric doctor, told me Conner would have to be transported by ambulance to his doctor's appointments in Dallas, which would be pretty frequent. He told me Conner wouldn't tolerate sitting in a car seat due to his brain injury. Dr. Sampson had not spent any time with Conner to see how he had become more and more alert. Conner smiled at us with his beautiful smile again. Dr. Sampson told me the less stimulation Conner got, the better it would be for him. I told him, *That's not true, Conner and I jam out every morning to Praise and Worship music. He absolutely loves it! Jamming didn't over stimulate him.* He disagreed with me and told me I needed to keep him in a dark, quiet room. His words broke my heart. I thought, this man hasn't paid attention to anything while we have been here! The blinds are open every day, and the sun is shining through.

The strong-willed person I am decided to prove Dr. Sampson wrong again! As soon as he walked out, I told mom I would be back. I went to Toys R Us to buy a car seat. I returned with the seat, and mom asked what my plan was. I said, *I am going to put Conner in this car seat in his bed and prove him wrong.* We put Conner in the car seat and sat the bed up all the way like he was strapped in the car. He immediately went to sleep after I strapped him all in. After an hour of him being sound asleep in the car seat, I got the doctor and told him I needed him to come to Conner's room. As he walked in, I asked him why he thought Conner would have to be transported by ambulance everywhere. He just threw his hands up and said, *Okay, point proven.* I can only imagine the talks about me that went on in their daily meetings. I really didn't care though, because my only concern was my child and what needed to be done for him. If Jesus said, *"faith can move mountains" (Matthew 17:20)*, we were going to choose to believe Him!

Home

When the sun peeked through the blinds in Conner's room on August third, I whispered a prayer of thanks to God. He knew this day would be difficult. I needed all the sunshine I could get. We were finally going home from the longest three months of my life. The ambulance transported us because of legal issues. When we got home, the facility had to make sure all of Conner's medical equipment had been installed and ready to use. I kept telling Conner we were finally going home, but it would be different since daddy and Adam wouldn't be there. I tried to hide how terrified I was about going home to face the giants in front of me.

I had so many emotions about going home. Kris had been my rock. I always counted on him to help figure things out. I had no clue how I was going to navigate life for Conner or me. I prayed the whole way home, *God, please give me the strength I need to endure all the things that lie ahead of me in this new life. There is no way I can do this on my own.*

As the ambulance pulled into my long driveway, my heart shattered. Along the driveway was a big banner Jennifer had made. The banner read, "Welcome Home Our Little Superman". Pulling up to the house, I was surprised to see a garage being built onto our home. People had donated their time and money to add the garage. What a blessing it was going to be. Now Conner would not be exposed to the weather. Many family and friends welcomed us home, definitely a sight to see. I was filled with so many mixed emotions.

The paramedics opened the ambulance doors to roll Conner out, and Mike B was standing there to greet us. Thankfully he had gone to Dallas and picked up all our belongings. Stepping out of the ambulance, I looked around and noticed how well kept my yard was. I expected to see overgrown grass. Mowing the lawn had not crossed my mind. It was amazing to know how much we were loved and cared about. Every need was met. What a blessing it was knowing so many people had been involved in taking care of our home, including our two dogs.

Walking into my house, filled with so many family and friends, I noticed two strange ladies in scrubs. I quickly realized they were with the nursing company. They walked up to introduce themselves, and reality started sinking in. I wanted to tell them to get out of my house, nothing against them personally. I was dreading everything I was about to face in life. The nurses explained all the equipment, medicine, how nursing would work and who my nurses would be. I was thinking, do I not get to interview the nurses and pick who I want? Instead, they already had them lined up for me. My house that once was my home, filled with my boys' joy and marital love, had become like a hospital. I had to figure out how to get the feeling of home back for Conner and me. To my surprise, our friend Will was in the process of redoing my kitchen countertops. Kris and I had planned on replacing the counters before the accident. I felt beyond blessed by all of the acts of service.

Conner's bedroom broke my heart. His baby bed had been taken down and replaced with a hospital bed. Reality set in more and more with each moment. Where are all of his toys? My little boy's room had been filled with medical equipment. My heart was beating about a million beats per minute as I tried holding in every emotion I was feeling. I didn't want Conner to know how upset and scared I felt. I despised everything about his room being turned into a hospital. He was getting close to being two years old, and his room was supposed to be filled with toys and fun things. I wanted to change his room as soon as I could!

Things wound down that evening, and all the guests left. I told my mom I didn't know how I would have strange people staying at my house. I was not leaving Conner in the hands of a nurse who knew absolutely nothing about his needs, not that night, not ever! Nurses only had a crash course on ventilators during school. Unless nurses had worked specifically with ventilator patients, they had no clue how to take care of the patients. Knowing how to care for a child on a ventilator is a life or death situation. Conner had to have breathing treatments every four hours around the clock.

I was mentally and physically exhausted. Mom told me to go lay down, and she would stay up all night and take the night shift. She rearranged every one of my kitchen cabinets that night just to stay awake. Leaving Conner's life in strange hands was not an option, but we didn't want to hurt the nurse's feelings.

I went to my bedroom and shut the door. I broke down crying. How was I supposed to sleep in the bed that Kris and I shared? I couldn't stand the thought of it. Am I really strong enough to handle all of this? I just want my family back! I was becoming mad. None of this is fair! I kept asking *why*! Why did God allow this to happen to our family? We had a beautiful and loving family. We were good people. There are so many bad people in the world. Why do bad things have to happen to good people? I ended up crying myself to sleep that night. I only slept a few hours. I wanted to make sure I was up when it was time to do Conner's treatments in case mom needed my help. I was afraid the nurse wouldn't be able to help her.

The next few days drug on. I was back on my emotional roller coaster. Grief had struck hard! It would have been easy to medicate myself to try and make my feelings numb. I knew that wouldn't be good for Conner or me. I was going to have to face the grief head-on. God would not leave my side and was carrying me through all my pain. Losing a husband, a child and having a second child needing intense medical care was way too much for one to bear without having God in their life.

My house was a revolving door of people coming and going. They were there with their love and support, which was a good thing for me. When the quietness settled in, the loneliness set in. My home that was once always full of noise and laughter of our boys playing was no longer! At night when everyone was gone, it got eerily quiet. Grief set in. Knowing as my friends and family walked out of my door, they could continue to experience life with their families. They would go on enjoying their kids or spouse, and I no longer could. Even though I was surrounded by people that loved me, I felt so alone. My heart was so broken.

Mom left her job so she could stay with us during the week. Dad or Donna would stay Saturday night, and they both would come out in the evenings after dad got off work. I had a great group of friends who stayed by my side through thick and thin. They all stepped up to the plate to help me. My friends Amy and Darah stayed some during the week to give my parents a break. Two other friends devoted staying on Friday nights. Erin stepped in and learned how to take care of all of Conner's medical needs. My step-sister, Tracy, and my nephew Reece would bring lunch out every Sunday afternoon and spend time with Conner. Kris's siblings and my nieces came on the weekends to love on Conner. All my other friends were faithful about coming by once a week to check on us. My friend Amanda was taking care of all the plants from the funeral. She was faithful not to let any of them die while we were in the hospital. Conner loved when my friend Brandy would stop by with her three kids. Her two girls, Aubrey, Josey and son Jack, doted all over Conner. The tragedy didn't just affect me, it changed my entire family's life. Life would never go back to the way it was before the accident. We all stuck together and did what we had to do for Conner.

Our church family went above and beyond to support us. We had meals served five days a week for two months. I was so spoiled. The home-cooked meals were amazing, and I was sad when the meals ended. Ladies from church came out in the afternoons to rock and play with Conner. I could get things like dishes and vacuuming done around the house. If the vacuum was running, I couldn't hear if his ventilator came off or if he needed to be suctioned. Conner loved his church lady time. Each lady had a specific day of the week she would came.

Edith, one of our church ladies and Conner's adopted Grandma, still comes every Thursday for Conner's Sunday School lesson. He gets so excited on Thursday knowing its Grandma Edith time. Edith and her husband, Grandpa Terry, plan a big Golf Tournament every year through our church for Conner. The tournament helps us pay for the additional medical costs we endure. Edith and the other church ladies have been such a blessing to Conner and me. Having a church family embrace you and knock down the doors of Heaven in prayer for you is powerful! God truly blessed me with an amazingly supportive family, friends, and church family.

Conner's body was still healing. Two people always had to be with him in the beginning. Everything was still new to us. It was terrifying when his oxygen levels would drop in a split second. Sometimes we had to suction out secretions from his trach for an hour, trying to get his oxygen levels back up. Our rural town didn't have all the medical professionals like at the hospital in Dallas. Trying to juggle my grief for Kris and Adam, on top of everything else, life had gotten overwhelming. Only by the Grace of God was I able to walk through the valley. There are so many days I didn't even want to get out of bed. Knowing I had to get up and take care of Conner kept me going. Conner kept me focused. I had to walk through the valley for Conner, but I knew God was always with me.

Shane came out almost every day during the week to do physical therapy with Conner. Conner started doing things I was told he would never do. For instance, when Shane assisted Conner in standing, Conner would lock his legs into place to stand. Conner was also responding to cold things. If we rubbed ice on his extremities, he would move them away from the ice. Shane did so many different physical therapy activities. I watched in amazement at how well Conner responded. Shane and Conner became really good buddies. Conner trusted Shane just as much as I did. The positive things in his therapy gave me much needed hope and encouragement.

I looked around the living room and saw our recent family pictures taken a couple of months before the accident. I longed for my family. It hurt unbearably to look at what had been, but it was a blessing to have the pictures. It helped me feel closer to Kris and Adam. We almost didn't get any good pictures that day because Conner was being a little stinker. My mom called the place we had the photographs taken, hoping they still had some of the proofs. They still had all the proofs! Usually, they deleted proofs after thirty days. It was another God thing.

There were many days I would lock myself in Adam's room, longing to feel close to him. I wouldn't allow anyone else in Adam's room after the accident. I didn't want anyone touching anything. I wanted him to wrap his little arms around my neck. I wanted to see him dressed in his Spiderman costume running through the house, shooting his web at us. Making us address him as Spiderman and not Adam.

Adam was the sweetest little boy who always made sure to tell me how much he loved me and how beautiful I was. He loved to sing and had an incredible voice for a little guy. Even his music teacher at school was impressed by his voice. He was the best big brother, very protective over Conner and loved him so much. Every morning when I would drop Adam off at school, he would want me and Conner to walk him in so everyone could see his little brother. Adam would give us both a kiss and a hug, and then Conner would throw a fit because he wanted to stay at school with Adam. I would ask Adam if he was sure he wanted us to walk him in because he knew Conner was going to throw a fit, and Adam always said yes. How I would love to have all of those moments back!! Adam wanted to be picked up from school with Conner in the car. He wanted to see his little brother the second he got out of school. Conner would get excited as he watched Adam walking to the car. My parents kept the boys for us so they wouldn't have to go to daycare while Kris and I worked. Looking back at life before the accident, I see many little things that we took for granted every day. Then when those moments are tragically removed, you long for those times again.

Conner took after me with his strong will and stubbornness. He was the little toddler you couldn't take your eyes off for even a split second. Conner loved being outside. He would sit at the front door, banging his head on the glass, crying because he wanted to go outside. He loved Adam and wanted to do everything his big brother did. Adam was so patient with him. Like any kid, Adam did have his moments when he wasn't patient. Conner started walking at eight months old. He wanted so badly to be able to keep up with Adam. There was a time when Conner threw a fit outside Adam's bedroom door. He was kicking and screaming because he wanted to play Nintendo with Adam. Finally letting Conner in, Adam unplugged one of the controllers and handed it to him. Conner plopped down next to his big brother and was perfectly content. He finally got his way!

One day when I locked myself in Adam's room, I walked into his Closet and turned the light on. I looked for something of his to hold to make me feel close to him. I was looking for his favorite spiderman toy. His toys were on the right side of the closet, and his clothes were on the left side. He had so many superhero toys! It was like finding a needle in a haystack with all of his superhero figurines.

I finally gave up looking for Spiderman and grabbed one of his shirts. I sat down on the floor of the small closet. I leaned up against the shelf where all his toys were. I buried my face into his shirt, crying uncontrollably. In frustration, I kicked my feet against the wall and cried out to God, asking if He was still with me. I felt alone and scared!

All of a sudden, something hit me in the head! I pulled my face from Adam's shirt. There was a brown leather binder lying on the floor. I tried to wipe some of my tears away so I could see through the blur. On the front were the words "Letters From Dad". I had been looking everywhere for the binder! Kris had started the "Letters From Dad" class four weeks before the accident. I was hoping that he had gotten to the letter-writing part and had written Conner a letter.

A smile comes over my face, and I let out a quiet chuckle. It was like Kris to hide the binder from me in Adam's closet. He knew I would never look for it in the closet. Kris knew I would snoop if he left it out where I could find it. My hands trembled as I started opening the binder. My heart skipped a beat at what I saw. There were two rough draft letters. One to me and one to my mom, definitely not what I expected. No wonder he hid the letters from me.

I started reading my letter and stopped for a minute to wipe the tears from my eyes. I read the first words, "To my beautiful wife". I could hear his voice speaking those words to me. I started reading the words, 'how proud he is to have me as his wife and mother to our two boys. How he loves that I always know the right answers and decisions when it comes to important things in our lives'. The rest of the letter, so intimate, so personal, for my eyes only.

After reading my letter from Kris, I said out loud, *God, thank you! Thank you for showing me you are still here with me, even though I know deep down inside you would never leave me. I just needed some reassurance today. Thank you for hitting me in the head with the binder! I needed to hear the words from Kris. I had often wondered over the last few months if Kris would have been proud of the decisions I had made. Thank you, God, for this extraordinary blessing today! It was what I needed!*

After a few nights, I couldn't handle sleeping in our bed anymore. It was heartbreaking to be without Kris. Sleeping in our bed alone without Kris killed me every time I had to get in it. It was depressing to walk into my almost-two-year-old son's bedroom. I couldn't stand Conner's room looking like a hospital room. I decided to buy us both new bedroom furniture.

There are so many things you wouldn't think would bother you until you lose someone. I had never really thought about what it would be like to see your loved one's shoes in their usual spot, knowing they would never put them on again. I had also not realized how much I took for granted the little things Kris did to help me around the house and with the boys. I didn't know how difficult it would be to sit at the kitchen table by myself and eat without being surrounded by my family. I wasn't ready to get rid of Kris's things. Knowing his clothes were hanging up in our closet helped me feel connected to him. I often walked into our walk-in closet, buried my head into Kris's clothes and cried into his shirts.

Kris was the love of my life, my best friend. I didn't think I would ever be able to love someone again. I thought there was no way possible to allow anyone else into my heart. Kris had my heart. I missed and needed him more than ever to comfort me. I found myself picking up the phone, dialing his number wanting to tell him something, then realizing that I couldn't call. He was no longer on earth to answer. I called anyway just to hear his voicemail.

I stayed in a constant state of prayer to give me the strength I needed. I was feeling defeated. August 23, 2006, my thirtieth birthday, I wanted to bypass it! I didn't feel like celebrating anything unless it was something about Conner. My friend Darah stayed the night with me the night before my birthday and slept in Conner's room so I could sleep.

Darah and mom came up with a plan for my birthday. Darah had gotten up while I was asleep and hid thirty index cards all over the house. The cards had birthday wishes written on them. I continued to find cards a week later. Mom told me she had been praying for God to give me a blessing for my birthday.

Shane came to do therapy and got Conner standing. Conner was little, it was easy to free stand him and not have to put him in a standing frame. I was in front of Conner, telling him what a good job he was doing. He picked his foot up and advanced it forward the best he could. I looked at Shane to see if I imagined it. Shane said, *I think he just took a step.* We asked Conner if he wanted to walk. I locked that knee in place, and we asked him to move his other foot forward, and he did. Conner continued to take steps like that for several minutes while helping him walk around the living room, supporting his upper body. I couldn't have asked for a better blessing on my birthday. I needed all the encouragement I could get. I didn't need a birthday present, Conner taking steps was the best present God could have given me. I cried happy tears instead of sad tears.

It was amazing to have so many people continue to keep praying for Conner. I had set up a blog while we were in the hospital to post updates about his condition. So many people from all over the world prayed for him and left comments on my post. It was encouraging to read the comments and see the love others had for us. Our community was unbelievable at embracing us as well.

The nursing situation was a nightmare at first. It was hard having a stranger in my house, and we had to train them on how to take care of Conner. Most of the nurses weren't consistent with coming on their days or would quit after a couple of weeks. I believe it was very overwhelming to them, plus I was very particular in how they did things. He was my number one priority. I wanted him taken care of correctly. Mom or I would stand over them to make sure they were doing things right.

We did have a couple of nurses who became like family, but it was still hard to always have someone in my home. I finally had gotten to a point where I didn't want to deal with the nursing stress. I ended up stopping the nursing service. I felt like I was running a hospital out of my house. Even though in reality I was, I had to figure out a new normal for Conner and me. I didn't want it to feel like a hospital all the time. I had plenty of help from my family, friends, and church family.

The garage was completed. Family and friends started stepping up to make some modifications to our home so that it would be a little more handicap accessible. A family member recruited others who gave their time and supplies to build a 20 x 20 living room. The original living room in our home wasn't big and was longer than it was wide. It made it a bit tight with all of Conner's equipment. The room was very much needed, and we lined it with tons of windows and glass patio doors. I wanted it to be nice and bright. Sunshine does a soul good! We were thankful for all the hard work and time people invested in making our house adjustments happen.

One Sunday afternoon, we fixed lunch for the gentleman working on the living room. As we sat at the table talking, I told one of them I felt bad he was working on a Sunday and not at church. He said, *This is my church for the day*. He was doing mission work and couldn't think of any better way of honoring God than to be the hands and feet for Him.

I didn't know how I was financially going to make it, but God took care of every single need. It reminds me of when Jesus said in Matthew 6:26 (NIV), *"Look at the birds of the air; they do not sow or reap or store away in barns, and yet your heavenly Father feeds them. Are you not much more valuable than they?* God promised to take care of us, and I had to trust in Him. I had to keep my focus on Conner while God kept his focus on me.

Survival was not an easy task. There was no rhyme or reason to how or when grief hits. There were so many days I felt like I was stuck in Groundhog Day. I didn't feel like smiling or being nice to anyone who walked through my door. I am thankful God placed the best group of friends and family in my life. It was hard to juggle all the feelings I went through. It was tough seeing them with their spouses and kids. If it wasn't for the love I had for them, I am afraid I would have closed my heart off to them. Praise God. He kept me from shutting them out of my life and allowed me to stay open to them loving on me. God knew each one of my friends brought something different I needed in my life.

Sometimes during Conner's treatment, I prepared his equipment and said silly things to see his sweet smile. Each day seemed the same in some ways, filled with doing treatments every four hours and therapy throughout the day. We were still trying to figure out how to manage all the care Conner required daily.

The summertime fun my friends looked forward to with their kids, I couldn't look forward to with Conner. My mind flashed back to the summer before, when Katrina and Caleb visited. We were all spending time at my dad's house in his pool, and the boys had so much fun swimming. Dad got in the pool and swam around with the boys at the shallow end. When I closed my eyes, I could hear the splashes and giggles. After our pool time, dad grilled burgers and hot dogs, such a special day! Before the accident, I was looking forward to spending a lot of time in dad's pool over the summer. The beeping of Conner's equipment brought my mind back to my current reality. I would give anything for Conner to be able to run, swim and play like he was just a few months ago. I started his breathing treatments and stroked Conner's head. I was so thankful I had him. I couldn't imagine coming into the house completely alone. Conner was my joy. I looked into his sweet face, and he smiled back at me. Every time I saw his sweet smile, my heart would be happy. Being able to see his smile made everything worth fighting for. Snuggling up to him when I was having a lousy day gave me such comfort.

Conner's two-year-old birthday was in September, and we were thankful he was home. Conner was home progressing and not the child the ICU doctors assured us he would be. My family helped me plan a big party to celebrate his life. We had so much to celebrate! Katrina and her family we able to fly in. We decided to go with a "Superman" theme because Conner was our little "Superman". We rented out a Community Building near our house and had a tremendous turnout. It was so incredible to see how many lives Conner had touched. During the party, Kris's little sister Amanda was sitting beside Conner and loving on him. She shared a memory with him about how Adam called her "Whatty" because he couldn't say, Aunt Amanda. That name had stuck with her.

We began settling into our new "normal". I missed feeling connected to my church family. I knew I could not go back to our couple's Sunday School. The thought of being there without Kris was too much. I loved our class. The Sunday school teachers were an older married couple. They had brought so much Christian marital guidance and love to our class. I didn't know where I would fit in anymore. I felt lost. It took me a while before I could walk back into our church sanctuary. Every time I considered going back, all I could picture was Kris and Adam's caskets at the front of the church. I would go into panic attacks just thinking about the funeral. I knew I would have to work through those memories to worship again in my home church.

Baltimore Rehab Facility

The strides Conner made with Shane's physical therapy was truly incredible. With Conner's responses from the hospital to therapy, his movements and reaction to pain, I recalled the conversation with my sister about the Kennedy Krieger Institute. A spinal cord rehab located in Baltimore, Maryland. I had put the possibility of going out of my mind because of the expenses. Katrina shared with me the Kennedy Krieger Institute was the best place in the country for spinal cord injuries. When she heard and saw all Conner was doing with Shane, she called and shared Conners story with the staff. They were very encouraging. They had just opened up their facility the prior year and worked with pediatrics on ventilators. Without even seeing the facility, I felt a little relief that we had found a place that specialized in spinal cord injuries. I realized then that even if we went and didn't feel like this facility was for us, it was essential to have a spinal cord specialist doctor.

Katrina suggested we go tour the Kennedy Krieger Institute. We both knew it would take a miracle to get Conner there. Once again, we both said, *We are going to have to choose faith over fear*. God had already performed one miracle with Conner's life. If He wanted us to get to Baltimore, we had to believe He would make a way. At the beginning of October, a couple of months after getting settled at home, my sister and I met at an airport in Baltimore to tour the Kennedy Krieger Institute. We were greeted by an RN and the Director of Care Management. Even though I had no answers to some of the questions, I was impressed at the questions she asked about Conner. We learned about a bone density test and a specific bowel regiment program. Most importantly, I was made aware of a condition called Autonomic Dysreflexia that could be life-threatening to an individual with a spinal cord injury. If they are in any kind of pain, even pain as simple as an ingrown toenail can cause Autonomic Dysreflexia, raising their blood pressure to the point it could cause a stroke. At that moment, we knew no matter what, we needed a doctor that specialized in spinal cord injuries. A specialist we didn't have access to in Texas or Oklahoma. We had every other specialist but not a spinal cord specialist.

As we toured the facilities gym, we were impressed by the intense physical and occupational therapy around us. The therapy techniques were amazing. The doctors were positive. They knew a spinal cord injury didn't define a patient and had seen how nerve pathways could be taught to bypass damaged nerves. They were excited to push their patients to see what all was possible for them to achieve. The possibilities for recovery at the Kennedy Krieger Institute were such a drastic change in mindset from the Kids Hospital's ICU floor. They never once spoke negatively of Conner's future. At the Kennedy Krieger Institute, their motto was "Hope through Motion". There is no false hope, they did not say bring your child here, and he will make a full recovery. Their message was to think outside the box. Their patients raved about the facility and their success with a restorative based therapy program. Up to that point, we had only heard of what Conner wouldn't be able to do. When we visited the Kennedy Krieger Institute, all we heard was, let's see what Conner "can" do.

As we left the facility, I said to Katrina, *That was like a breath of fresh air*. I had new hope. I felt excited about the Kennedy Krieger Institute! We called our parents who were watching Conner and shared about all we had seen and heard. They were filled with hope at the possibilities too. I felt in my heart we found the place that Conner needed. However, we already knew the insurance would not cover the facility. We would have to raise money to get him there. Our first trip there would be better as an inpatient so they could get to know Conner. I wasn't excited about the idea of staying inpatient after being in the hospital for so long. I understood if we stayed, the doctors could evaluate him better. We scheduled our first appointment for the first of July 2007, which gave us about ten months to raise money.

We made plans on how to raise money because the rehab was going to be very expensive. Getting to the Kennedy Krieger Institute almost seemed impossible with all the other out of pocket medical expenses.

We chose to believe God would provide the money we needed. Katrina, from North Carolina, orchestrated a big fundraiser. News stations did stories. Our amazing community and surrounding communities embraced our goal to get Conner to Maryland. We saw baseball teams put together tournaments for Conner. There were pop up bake sales and car washes. People were even making anonymous donations to Conner's medical fund. My family and friends worked hours on the big fundraiser while there were so many other fundraisers going on all over town. Several local schools did coins for Conner, where students brought in spare change. There were basketball tournaments, pie auctions, baked potato fundraisers, golf tournaments, and the list goes on. We were beyond grateful for the way our community stepped up to help. With each event, we got closer to our goal. God stirred people's hearts to be a part of what He was doing in Conner's life. Each event, big or small, infused hope into our lives. Even though days were still emotionally hard for Conner and me, I learned the true meaning of Romans 12:2 (NIV) *"Be joyful in hope, patient in affliction, faithful in prayer"*.

Emergency Trip to Dallas

One of those hard days came just a couple of weeks into October. Conner started having breathing issues. We talked with the pulmonologist and made changes to his breathing treatments. Over the next few days, Conner continued to worsen and struggled to breathe even when we gave him oxygen, which he had not required up to that point. We took him to our local ER, knowing they wouldn't be able to do much for him. He needed to be back in Dallas. Conner had gotten so bad I didn't feel like we could drive him to Dallas. He needed to be airlifted. The medical team on the helicopter was not trained on ventilators, so I was allowed to fly with them. I was thankful they allowed me to go. I couldn't imagine letting Conner go without me. My parents drove and met us in Dallas.

I had to sit on the opposite side of Conner behind the pilot. One lady was in the middle, and a man on the other side of her at Conner's head. I couldn't see Conner's face but could see his oxygen and heart rate levels. We all had radio headphones on in case they needed to talk to me. As I was looking out over the night sky, I was thinking about how much I dreaded going back to the hospital. Suddenly, a voice came over the radio asking, *What does low pressure mean on the ventilator?* I responded, *Make sure the ventilator is still connected to his trach.* His oxygen went so low, Conner crashed. I watched his oxygen levels get into the twenties, and his heart rate into the twenties. I watched them start CPR compressions, and my heart stopped. I was terrified and wanted to move them out of my way to take care of him myself. All I knew to do was pray. I prayed, begging God to save Conner and not let him die in that helicopter. Then, a calming peace swept over me, the peace of God.

After a couple of minutes, they had Conner's vitals back up. His ventilator had come off his trach, and with Conner having the breathing issues, his body couldn't compensate. It's incredibly terrifying to watch someone do chest compression on your child and feel completely

108

helpless. The medical professionals on that helicopter later took ventilator classes.

As we landed at the hospital in Dallas, my legs were completely weak from the horrifying experience. As Conner was being unloaded, I tried my best to be patient and get to Conner as the medical professionals were on the helicopter pad waiting and trying to get a report. I finally just pushed through to get to Conner. I knew he had to be terrified, and he couldn't hear or see me on the helicopter. I wanted him to see me and give him some comfort. Sure enough, when I got to him, his eyes looked as though he was full of fear. When he locked his eyes on me, he started pouting. I kissed him and told him *Mommy is here.*

The pilot asked me if I was okay, I told him I would be when my nerves calmed down. He told me he was proud of me because they were used to landing the helicopter to calm others down. I told him, *Panicking wouldn't help Conner, and I needed their focus on him, not me. Besides, all I knew to do was to pray.*

As we made our way into the ER room, hoping my parents would get there soon, it was taking everything in me not to break down. I knew I needed to be strong for Conner. Thankfully Billie, who lived in Dallas, was there waiting on us. It was nice to see a familiar face. The moment my mom walked into the room, I told her I needed a minute. They didn't even have a clue about what had happened. Stepping out into the hallway, I allowed my emotions to take over. I had held it in as long as I could. The helicopter pilot was filling my family in on what happened. Praise God, Conner only had an upper respiratory infection and was only hospitalized for a week.

Holidays

The holidays were right around the corner, and I couldn't imagine how we were going to celebrate. The pain of losing Kris and Adam was still raw to me. I knew the holiday season was going to be hard for me. Doing our normal traditions without Kris and Adam was unimaginable. I finally concluded I wasn't going to celebrate. I told my family, *I'm sorry, I just can't handle the pain of holidays this year*. Conner was still young, and he wouldn't even know he was missing out on the holidays.

There was no need for everyone to put off celebrating because of the pain I was enduring. I had no plans of putting my Christmas tree up or exchanging Christmas gifts. I asked others to honor my wishes and not give us presents. That isn't what Christmas was about. It was about the birth of our Lord and Savior, and we would celebrate the Birth of Jesus Christ, just not the usual traditional way. I wasn't sure that I would ever be able to do things like we used to. I wasn't sure what our holiday tradition would be in the future.

God took care of Christmas for us. Our pulmonologist, Dr. Longhorn, was ready to try vent weaning with Conner again. Conner was still over-breathing the ventilator. The weaning process required another inpatient stay at The Rehab and Training Facility. I asked if we could do it over Christmas. At first, he questioned my decision. He said, *Usually, no one would want to be in the hospital over Christmas*. I told him I couldn't bear the thought of being home during Christmas this year. He agreed, and we ended up back in the same room we were in before with the little baby girl roommate still there. Being at The Rehab and Training Facility was a good reason and distraction for me to be away from home.

Conner did well with the vent weaning. He wasn't strong enough to come completely off the vent during that time. We were able to put all of the ventilator settings as low as they could go. I felt like it was a mind thing with Conner. He was conditioned and addicted to the ventilator since he had been on it for several months. His lungs were much stronger than they were in the beginning. We had already started weaning him off some of his breathing treatment medicine. His breathing treatments went to every eight hours from four.

I had developed a great relationship with our two pulmonologists. We saw them once a month in the beginning. They were very well involved in our care. I trusted them, and they began to trust me. I am sure doctors don't always experience a stubborn, strong-willed mom who doesn't back down if something doesn't feel right about the treatment and procedures. Having all of the support that I had played an enormous role in Conner's care.

Love and Adventures

New Love

God is so amazing to have our whole life orchestrated before we are even conceived! When I lost Kris, I believed my heart would never be healed enough to give it to someone else. My heart belonged to him, and I wasn't sure I would ever be able to love someone again. Thankfully God had different plans for my life. God's timing is always right.

My journey with Robbin started almost a year after the accident. His sister, Keri, owned a boutique/tanning salon in our town, and we had become friends. One night while I was there, Keri invited me to an Easter play that her church was putting on. Needing a break, I decided to go with my friend Nicole. We were amazed at how good the play was. Robbin was in charge of all the props and also played the soldier beating Jesus with a whip. As I watched him beat Jesus, tears began flowing down my cheek. I was thinking to myself of the scripture "by his stripes we *are healed*". At that moment, I knew God was going to heal me from all of the pain and tragedy I had suffered.

When the play was over, Keri brought Robbin out to where Nicole and I were. She introduced us. Robbin asked, *Well, what did you guys think of the play*? I responded, *It was terrific, and you guys did such a great job acting it out*. We talked for a little while. He asked me how Conner was. I told him Conner was good, and I invited him to the fundraiser we were having in two weeks. Still not being too sure about all of this, I tried not to linger very long. I laugh now because to this day, he can still describe what I was wearing that day!

April 14 came, and it was time for our first of many big fundraisers. My sister flew in, and we were supposed to have a big Kid's Day in the Park, but the weather got bad, and we had to re-direct the activities to our local High School Gym. Since we had to change our plans so quickly, my sister contacted the local radio stations and asked if they could help us spread the word. We went to the radio station and did an online interview. They invited my sister to stay for the next several hours and continue sharing about the event between songs. I was surprised they gave us so much air time. All four of our radio stations in Ardmore were housed in this building so that she could get the word out on all four stations. All of our vendors were able to transition to the school. We had many activities planned from college athletes there signing autographs, silent auction items, food, bouncy houses, face painting, musicians playing, kids games, and our mayor claiming it Conner McDougall Day.

Robbin said he was driving down the road when he heard one of the commercials about our fundraiser. He said he felt like God was pulling on his heart and that he needed to go. He reached out to Keri and got my phone number. I'll never forget getting a text from him that day, asking if he was still invited to come to the fundraiser. Of course, I said yes. I told him I would also have him a Super Conner t-shirt waiting for him at the door so he could wear it during the fundraiser. We had shirts made up for sale that had a superman symbol with a C in the middle instead of an S. Being one tuff little boy, Conner indeed had become everyone's little superman. That was about the extent of the conversation that day.

Many people were excited to meet Conner in person. It turned out to be a very successful day. With this event and all the other fundraisers going on, we had enough money to take Conner to Baltimore. I'll be honest, I doubted in the beginning. I thought raising enough money to get Conner to Maryland would be impossible. I learned through this to never doubt what God can do. I knew better than to doubt Him. I had already seen Him do the impossible with Conner. We can be *mountain movers* when we put our trust in God!

Robbin showed up at the fundraiser that day ready to help out. Luckily some ladies he graduated with were there as volunteers. He was able to talk with them and not feel entirely out of place. It was a crazy day. I was busy with the news media and everything going on. We didn't have much time to talk. I know my family was trying to figure out who he was and why he was around Conner and me the whole day.

114

At the end of the event, Mom and Choc decided to take Conner home. Conner was pretty worn out from all the attention. It was such a busy day, we never even stopped to eat. After we finished cleaning things up, Robbin asked if I would like to get something to eat. I remember he offered to take me anywhere I wanted to go. Quickly I replied, Burger King. He was a little thrown back from my choice and even chuckled. I remember him asking, *are you sure you want Burger King?* I definitely was sure. I was starving and didn't want to wait forever to eat. Now we laugh that technically our first date was Burger King.

Sitting there talking over fries and cheeseburgers, I realized he was easy to talk to, and we both had the same values in life. I knew I needed to get back home to relieve my mom, but I didn't want the conversation to end. I decided to invite Robbin to the house so we could talk more. I told him to give me about an hour before he got there. I knew I needed to get my mom gone before he arrived. I didn't want to have a conversation with her about who he was yet. I wasn't even sure that my heart was ready for anything. Katrina was staying the night with me and would be getting there about the same time as Robbin. I knew it would be easier to explain our friendship to her at that point.

Losing your spouse isn't like a divorce. I was still madly in love with Kris and unsure if my heart was ready to allow another man in. The knock at the door caused me to have mixed emotions. Part of me was a little excited. The other part felt like I was cheating. Opening the door, his smile was contagious. I was still unsure of where this might lead. I caught a smile spreading across my face. We sat in my living room and talked. I shared with him all the things God was doing in our lives. He heard all about the things we had been through, not just the good but the bad as well. He asked questions and was truly curious about everything. Honestly, I figured after that night, I wouldn't hear from him again. My life was pretty intense. I thought having a special needs child while grieving Adam and still being in love with Kris would have run him off. But instead, it had the complete opposite effect.

Robbin told me that it was the love I had for Kris and my faith in God that drew him closer to me. Due to circumstances out of his control, Robbin's first marriage ended. After being single for two years, Robbin started contemplating the thought of marriage again. While in prayer, Robbin gave God a very specific list of what he wanted in a wife. He honestly didn't think he would ever find anyone that crossed off half of the list, much less complete the list. Then he met me. He said I checked off every one of the boxes. Robbin also had two boys that he had custody of. Colton, who was eight and a second one who has requested to remain anonymous in this book. We both agreed we wouldn't bring his son around until we knew where this was going. My house was a revolving door of family and friends coming in to help me. Conner was used to so many people coming in and out of our home. We introduced Robbin to Conner as a new friend. We knew we needed to take things slow. Robbin didn't want to push me if my heart wasn't ready. He knew I had enough heartache already in my life.

I knew Robbin also needed to soul search and make sure that stepping into our lives with all of Conner's needs was something he thought he could handle. Conner was my first priority, and that wouldn't be changing. I also had to make sure that I was ready to let him into my heart and that my heart was ready to have a new child in my life. Colton was in the same grade as Adam. I knew that this would be a challenge for me watching Colton do all the things that Adam should have been doing. Also, was my heart genuinely going to be able to handle watching Colton experience life like a normal kid when I so desperately wanted Conner up experiencing life the same way?

I prayed very hard about Robbin. I told God if he wasn't meant to be in mine and Conner's life, then show me that. If he isn't, then remove him graciously because I knew Robbin was an amazing guy. I didn't want to ruin the friendship we had going.

As May quickly approached, I struggled. Adam's birthday was Thursday, May 10, 2007, and Mother's Day was the following Sunday.

116

The one year anniversary of the accident was the nineteenth. I wondered how I would be able to mentally survive throughout the month.

On Adam's birthday, I needed to get away from everything. The pain of being home with memories was making the day harder. Robbin offered to take Conner and me to a local animal park. It was a big cat sanctuary, and he thought Conner would like how up close we could get to the animals. Unknown to Robbin at the time, this place held a soft place in my heart. Adam's class had taken a field trip to this zoo, and Kris had gone as a sponsor. During the trip, Kris had used our camcorder to film Adam and his friends as they made their way around the zoo. One of the funniest parts of the video was Kris trying to get the boys on film in front of a big lion named Mufasa. Mufasa must have been cranky that day. He ran up and attacked the fence and roared loudly. Of course, this sent the boys racing away. The funny part was hearing Kris, my big strong husband, screaming like a girl in the microphone of the recorder. I never let him live that down.

My heart was broken that day, not being able to celebrate what would have been Adam's seventh birthday. I again found myself questioning why God allowed the tragedy to happen to my family. It wasn't fair! I didn't get enough time with Adam and Kris. We had so much more in life we wanted to experience together. I knew that for the rest of my life, there was always going to be this huge void and heartache for them. I don't think anyone can ever get over the loss of a loved one, especially the loss of your child. I eventually had to learn to live again and manage the pain, but the pain never went away. One day we will all be reunited in Heaven again, and what a glorious day that will be! I was so thankful when that day finally came to an end. I couldn't bear the reality anymore of not getting to celebrate Adam's birthday with him! I just wanted to close my eyes and start a new day.

The first anniversary hit me like a ton of bricks. The weight was so heavy on my heart. I couldn't believe it had been a year since I heard Kris and Adam's voices, felt their touch and seen Conner actually running around the house. The night before the anniversary, I was restless. I couldn't get any sleep. The only thing running through my mind was that horrible day. I laid there, wishing I could go back in time and change the outcome of that day. I knew Kris and Adam would never want to come back from glory. I can't even begin to imagine what they are experiencing in heaven. To this day, I still daydream about what they are in Heaven doing. When I get sad, I get peace remembering where they are and who they are with. We can only imagine what heaven is like!

My friends, Mike and Stephanie, were aware of the anniversary and asked if we could get together to keep my mind busy. I agreed. I thought that was a great idea. Erin swung by my house and picked Conner and me up, so I wouldn't have to drive alone. Arriving at Mike and Stephanie's, I noticed there were several cars in the driveway. They had invited others to join us. Even Robbin was there. I lived in gratitude, knowing that so many people loved me and wanted to make sure that I was okay. We hung out and loved on Conner, which made the day a little easier to bear, keeping my mind busy.

When we were back home that evening, the house was quiet. It was those times that were the hardest. I wrote Kris and Adam letters. I found that writing them letters was great therapy. It gave me a way to pour my heart and soul out to them both. Dad had put a mailbox up at the cemetery, and I sealed my letters and placed them in it. I don't like to wish my life away, but May has too many heartaches, and it is a month I always dread to see coming. I am still so thankful to see the month of May go.

Kennedy Krieger Institute

June 24, 2007, we had planned for our two-week stay, and we packed the car full. We could barely fit anyone in the car. The Oklahoma heat was so intense, I shouldn't have put on make-up. I had sweated most of it off while loading the car. I didn't care, I was excited to be going to Baltimore, Maryland, with my parents, stepparents and sister. A trip I thought would be impossible, God made it possible! My stepsister, Tracy, reached out to a local organization and asked if they would fly us to Baltimore on their corporate jet. The organization offered to fly us for free, and we would land in Maryland before nightfall. Another unexpected blessing from God! Flying Conner on a commercial plane would have been expensive and nearly impossible.

I couldn't wait for my parents to see the facility! They would be excited about the progress Conner would have over the next two weeks at the Kennedy Krieger Institute. Unpacking the plane, loading, and unloading the rental car, we were exhausted by the time we were checking in and settling into our room. Even though my first visit to see the facility was very positive, I had mixed emotions. I was getting nervous and concerned they wouldn't believe in Conner. I was concerned they would see Conner only through the lens of what the medical textbooks expected of a quadriplegic and not through a lens of belief. I was so afraid our stay would end up the same as the ICU. I would have been devasted if it did. I needed some encouragement in our lives about Conner's future. We were all excited about this new chapter of life. I prayed God would allow great things to happen while we were inpatient for two weeks at the Kennedy Krieger Institute.

Our first morning, we were all excited to see what was in store for Conner! We rode up the elevator and walked through the doors to the therapy gym. We were once again amazed by all the equipment they had for their patients. I was amazed at watching what they did with other patients in the spinal cord therapy gym. Conner's first day was full of evaluations as they checked to get a baseline on all he could do. They were highly impressed with Conner's physical condition. Conner was in good physical condition because of Shane's guidance and diligence with physical therapy at home.

The Kennedy Krieger Institute was like a summer camp for Conner! He had so many exciting pieces of therapy equipment at his disposal. Monday through Friday, the therapist worked four hours a day doing physical and occupational therapy. Watching Conner push hard was overwhelming to me. In his eyes, I could see the determination to want to do everything they were asking of him. Even though he was tired and worn out at times, here was my two-year-old toddler doing four hours of therapy a day. I exercise for forty-five minutes and think I am about to pass out. I was so proud of him for pushing through. The therapists knew how to make therapy so much fun for kids, which made a huge difference. There were times they had to get creative. Conner was more interested in watching everyone else in the gym. They had to find other rooms to work with him where there weren't so many distractions. He was a toddler, keeping him on track for 4 hours a day was an accomplishment in itself.

We had a meeting with the head clinical director Dr. McDonald who started the Spinal Cord Injury Clinic at the Kennedy Krieger Institute. As I sat across from him, I was so incredibly thankful God had provided a way for us to get to the facility! They spoke life over Conner and operated with a motto of *"Hope through Motion."* He had already gone over all of Conner's MRIs, CT scans, and medical records. Despite knowing their slogan, I was a little nervous walking into this room, praying he didn't tell us there was no hope for Conner. I had watched Conner move and do things in therapy that I never expected to see. I had hope.

As my family and I sat down at the big oval wood table in the conference room, Dr. McDonald and his nurse practitioner walked in. He was so friendly and down to earth. He showed us Conner's scans and explained more in-depth about the injury. He told us if you had to have a spinal cord injury, you want it to happen at Conner's age. All of his nerves had not completely formed, which gave him a better chance of recovery. He may not make a full recovery, but he could possibly regain back some of his movement. Only the future and hard work would determine his recovery down the road. He even told us that there might be a cure for spinal cord injuries one day, but if your body isn't in good physical shape, you wouldn't be a candidate. Dr. McDonald did not give us any false hope, but it was nice to finally hear some positive news.

Keeping Conner active was going to be huge for his lungs, heart, and his skin health, so he didn't end up with skin breakdown causing wounds. It was also good for his bone density since as a toddler, he needed lots of weight-bearing for his bones to grow correctly. The usual weight-bearing toddlers get was one of the downfalls to him being injured so young.

It is amazing how God designed our bodies to grow. We don't think about this until something like a spinal injury happens and interrupts the whole process. Activity-Based Restorative Therapy is the type of therapy found at the Kennedy Krieger Institute. It is used to find ways to restore your function and sensation. Rather than compensating for your loss, Activity-Based Restorative therapy aims to restore as much of your normal function as medically possible.

The Kennedy Krieger Institute came up with a plan over our two-week stay. They sent us home with a detailed notebook of all the new therapy to do from home. They did electrical stimulation to every muscle group and had him do a fun activity involving those muscles. The stimulation sends the signal back up to his brain, telling the brain this is how you use that particular muscle group.

Robbin and his son Colton surprised us and flew up to Baltimore. Robbin said he was really curious about the Kennedy Krieger Institute. I think he just missed me. He had booked a hotel on the outskirts of Baltimore, and just like a man, he hadn't even looked at a map. The hotel was at least an hour away, so I canceled his reservations. I booked him a room in the same hotel my parents stayed at, and he hasn't booked a hotel since.

The Kennedy Krieger Institute closed on July fourth. We took Conner to the hotel on the night of the third. Dad and Donna decided to go to Washington, D.C. to watch the firework show there, and Katrina had flown home to be with her family. Baltimore did a firework show in the inner harbor, and since we were only a couple of blocks away, we decided it would be awesome to walk down and watch them. There was a slight chance of rain, so we carried umbrellas, and just as we were settled in a nice spot, the heavens opened up, and it began to rain. Robbin took off running with Conner and found a dry spot under an awning. We all huddled together for a few minutes coming up with a plan to get back to the hotel. Luckily mom is always prepared and had packed some cheap disposable ponchos in Conner's supply bag. We don't go on ANY adventures without ponchos now. We wrapped Conner and his wheelchair in the ponchos. All you could see of Conner was his little face and a huge smile, the boy loves adventure! Robbin started pushing Conner with Colton close behind, and they ran all the way back to the hotel. Mom and I used the umbrellas and made our way back as quickly as we could. We all looked like drenched cats, not a dry place on us, except for Conner. He was snug as a bug and still smiling. The rain finally stopped, and the firework show started. We all gathered up on the balcony of one of the rooms and watched the beautiful display. That was the first of a long list of epic adventures our family took together.

The last two days at the **Kennedy Krieger Institute**, mom and I started doing the therapy so the therapist could make sure we did it correctly. If you don't go home and follow through with the therapy, they told us that you would not see results. They told us Conner would benefit the best if we could come every six months for two-week outpatient therapy. The same concept, four hours of physical and occupational therapy, Monday through Friday. We just wouldn't have to stay inpatient. Being outpatient would cut the cost down for us, and it would make Conner happier. He didn't like staying inpatient. It's hard to sleep in a hospital-like facility.

I wasn't sure how we would continue to pay for the therapy, but I knew if it was in God's will, He would provide the way. I was also going to start working on our insurance company to cover the service since there was no facility in Oklahoma or Texas for pediatric ventilator patients.

We had enough money left from our big fundraiser to get back to Baltimore two more times. I went ahead and scheduled for the following year. Since we went in July, six months later would be in the winter. We didn't want to be in Baltimore when it snowed, so we scheduled the next session for April 2008.

For the next nine months, we worked hard with Conner. Shane continued to come and incorporate what the **Kennedy Krieger Institute** included in our home workout plan. We started to see Conner come alive. It was the encouragement I needed to see.

Our physical therapist, Brooke, ended up being with us from here on out. We love all of our therapists, they are like family. They all hold a special place in our hearts. They know how to keep Conner going and motivated. Conner has grown to trust and love them and gets excited when it is time to go back to Baltimore. Conner has even nicknamed one of them Mrs. Anything. Conner sleeps with a sock monkey named patches every night that Mrs. Anything gave him.

It was always amazing watching Conner pushing hard through therapy when some of the other young kids were crying and wanting no part of it. Conner still has such a spirit of strength and courage. He still works hard in therapy. Every day, Conner inspired me to continue to push forward.

As he got a little older, one of Conner's favorite activities was playing video games and bowling during therapy. Mrs. Scrapple, one of his OT's, made this possible for Conner. It was so much fun to see him doing activities many of the kids his age could do. They were able to hook the video game device up to his hand, and they would work with his eye and hand control, allowing Conner to actually play the game himself. His smile was so big as we cheered him on! Another one of our

Occupational Therapist, that recently had a baby boy, used painting as a therapy. She also introduced Conner to virtual reality.

I never get tired of seeing him roll over! That may seem like a small feat, but it's something the ICU doctors had assured me would never happen. Every time he rolled himself over, we erupted in cheers! Not sure if he loved us cheering for him or just loved to see his therapist smile. I think he loved seeing them get so excited for him. The Kennedy Krieger Institute is the most positive place I had ever taken Conner! As Conner works out, you can watch kids, teens and adults doing therapy all around the room. The therapist pushes each person to go beyond what they think they can do and are their biggest cheerleaders!

There are so many times we wish money wasn't an issue, and we could stay longer at the Kennedy Krieger Institute. Even though we work hard with Conner at home following their home workout plan. They have top of the line equipment that we can't afford to get at home. They also have the knowledge and expertise. It is a blessing and miracle God has continued to provide a way for us twice a year.

Many amazing things have happened at the Kennedy Krieger Institute over the years. One of my favorite things was seeing Conner walking with the G-EO robotic walker. Brooke decided to try it out on Conner. Seeing my little boy standing and walking even with a robotic walker was one of the happiest days of my life. I had lots of happy tears! Conner loved every minute of it as well. Even though it was hard work for him, his smile said it all. Unfortunately, we haven't been able to do it again due to a tight hamstring muscle we have been working on. Conner went through a big growth spurt. Spinal cord injuries make it hard for the muscle and bone to grow fast without the weight-bearing he needs. We are working on it so we can hopefully get him back on the G-EO in the future.

Brooke, did a case study on Conner that she presented in Nashville, Tennessee. The case study was on how doing Activity Based Restorative Therapy and following through with it at home truly makes a difference in a high-level spinal cord injury in their overall health. Conner has had some health issues over the years, but nothing like the medical books said he would. Some of his health issues weren't due to his spinal cord injury. God led our path to the Kennedy Krieger Institute to get the knowledge and care he needs. It has been a game-changer for Conner's life.

The Kennedy Krieger Institute has taught us all that God has designed the human body to be able to heal itself! When you see a loved one doing things they were never supposed to do, it's so uplifting and encouraging! He has regained movement in his upper extremities. Every time Conner moves, I just think how amazing our God is! Conner can roll from his side to his back using his arms, even with his weak upper extremities. He has an RTI leg and arm bike with a motor on it that helps him cycle. Conner is hooked up to electrical stimulation on his muscle groups that help to strengthen the muscles. This retrains the signal to the brain that this is how you move your legs or arms. He goes anywhere from three to nine miles on his leg bike. Sometimes, when Conner uses the arm bike, he starts kicking his legs at the same time. The first time he kicked his legs, it scared me. I wasn't sure why all of a sudden this was happening. I reached out to our occupational therapist in Baltimore, and she told me that it is exciting news. That means the signal is getting through to his legs. We know over the years that all the hard work we have done is paying off little by little. We don't know what the future holds. I would love to see him up walking and running again. I don't know that it will happen on this side of heaven, but I will never stop praying for that miracle. We have already witnessed so many miracles.

Pool therapy is an excellent therapy for people with spinal cord injuries. A year after the accident, we figured out a way to get Conner into the pool, despite the ventilator. This took a lot of planning. The first time we got Conner into the pool, he was so relaxed. The water takes the pressure off of his body. It is a lot easier for Conner to move in the pool. Conner loved pool therapy so much that this has become part of his therapy routine in the summer.

There are many things that Kennedy Krieger Institute has been impressed with over the years with Conner. Since Conner has such a high-level spinal cord injury, and it happened at such a young age, there should be things we should have had issues with over the years. One of them being scoliosis. Most kids who were injured with lower injuries have had several surgeries for scoliosis. This is where your spine curves due to a lack of back muscles to keep your spine straight. Not until his teen years did we start to see some scoliosis. It isn't bad enough to need surgery. Our orthopedic specialist said Conner might never need surgery. As long as it doesn't get any worse, we are good. I take it to heart when something goes wrong with Conner. Especially spine issues. I feel like it is my fault. Our Spinal Cord specialist doctor, Dr. Sadowsky, in Baltimore is so sweet and caring. She looked at his spine and commented about the slight scoliosis. Tears filled my eyes. I don't like things to go wrong with Conner. Dr. Sadowsky told me it was okay, it was a miracle he hadn't shown signs of this before now. She told me it wasn't bad but something we needed to stay on top of. They are all so patient and caring with us there.

We are usually at the Kennedy Krieger Institute during Halloween. All of the therapists, medical staff, and patients dressed up. Since we don't take Conner trick or treating, I decided to start going all out on his Halloween costumes. This way, it made Halloween fun for him. I love it when I come up with an idea, and Robbin and his father, Dale, can make it happen. The Kennedy Krieger Institute staff told us that their Halloween highlight is waiting to see Conner's costume. I always keep it a surprise. When I say we go all out, I mean we go all out. Conner's wheelchair is no longer a wheelchair. It becomes the main part of the costume. He has been a monkey in space with the wheelchair being a space shuttle, the Red Barron with the wheelchair being a tri-plane, Batman with the wheelchair being the batmobile, and my personal favorite Darth Vader with the wheelchair being T-wing fighter. Conner loves getting to show off his Halloween costume every year!

Due to a generous donor we got to stay the entire month of November at the Kennedy Krieger Institute. Since the trip was so close to

Thanksgiving, we arranged for most of our family to meet us in Baltimore to spend Thanksgiving touring Washington, D.C. We were really excited about doing this together. Robbin's parents, Dale & Pam came and brought Colton. Robert and Katrina came along with Caleb and Kaitlyn. All of the kids were finally old enough to handle the walking we would need to do around Washington, D.C. Conner loves being around family.

Thanksgiving morning, we woke up and had not figured out where we were going to eat our Thanksgiving meal. We weren't worried about it though, we were just excited to go see the Smithsonian museums and the monuments! We packed a lot into the day. There were times it took three of us to push Conner at Arlington National Cemetery! Conner thought it was funny we had to work so hard to get him up the hills. We were able to fit in so much in one day! We had a lot of fun! Outside the Air and Space Museum we saw an oasis! A street filled with Food Trucks! We were all so hungry. Eating our Thanksgiving Meal out of food trucks sounded wonderful! One truck was even offering a special "Thanksgiving Turkey Sandwich" with cranberry sauce on it. It may have been a little cool eating outside, but our bodies were thankful for the replenishment. We had so many steps already and it was only lunch time. Conner loved the Air and Space Museum. He enjoyed seeing the space shuttles and planes hanging from the ceiling.

Marriage

Robbin is so patient. He stood by me through all the new roads I was navigating. My family wasn't the most welcoming to him in the beginning. Dad and Donna were nice but apprehensive of a new man in mine and Conners life. Choc wouldn't even talk to him. We would be in the house having a conversation, and with Robbin standing beside him, Choc would look at me and say stuff like *Tell the yard boy he needs to get the leaves off the back porch before they become a fire hazard.* Choc had made up several names for Robbin like Yard Boy, Pool Boy, whatshisface, and that guy. Mom was cordial but was standoffish. The role he was stepping into, Robbin had really big shoes to fill. Mom told him she wouldn't shake his hand until she was sure he was the one. My family loved Kris like their own son. Kris's dad left when Kris was very young. His mom died of cancer the summer before his senior year. My parents became his parents, and it was tough for them to see another man take Kris's place. My parents had also watched me go through so much heartache and pain. They didn't want anyone coming in and breaking my heart.

Kris's family was just the opposite. They got to meet Robbin at Conner's third birthday party. Robbin was nervous about meeting them. One by one, they came in, and I introduced him. By the end of the party, I had all of their blessings. By Christmas 2007, Robbin and Colton had already been added to the list of names that we draw out for presents. Robbin is now referred to as "Brother-n-Law" by Kris's siblings and "Uncle" by their children. Colton now refers to them as his McDougall family.

As time moved on, I began falling in love with Robbin. His passion for God and seeing the father he was, made me love him even more. I would not be with anyone who didn't put God first in their life. So thankful his parents, Dale and Pam, had raised him to be such a great man of God. He quickly learned how to take care of Conner and embraced him like his own. If we follow God's plan for our lives, the happiness we can find along the way is amazing. That doesn't mean it won't always be easy. I am in awe when I think about how before Robbin and I were conceived, God knew that we both would be each other's "happily ever after" one day.

I was beginning to think we would never get engaged. I think Robbin was just trying to make sure I was ready for that next step in our life. After a little over two years of dating, he finally proposed to me. It was the fourth of July, we were on a beach, watching the sun set. As I was watched the sun dance across the water, Robbin wrote, "Will you marry me" in the sand. I turned around to find him on one knee with a ring in his hand and a smile across his face.

Before Robbin proposed, he asked my parents for my hand. After a stern talk, Dad and Donna gave him their blessings. When he asked mom and Choc, it was a different story. Mom told Robbin that before she would say yes, she had a couple of questions for him. She pulled out a notebook, there was a list of questions on three different pages. Mom went through her questions one by one, Robbin answered them. At the end of the questions, mom reached out her hand and shook Robbin's. Choc told him no, and if we went through with it, he would be standing outside the church with a shotgun. Of course, Choc was joking. By this time, Choc had warmed up to Robbin!

We had so many friends and family who prayed for our relationship. They prayed for me to find love again after the accident. We decided to do a big wedding. We wanted to celebrate with everyone. Our good friend and associate pastor Todd married us. Todd had started as the Young Adults Minister when the accident happened. Todd and his wife Kim had walked this journey with us.

August 15, 2009, we merged our families together to make one beautiful family under the covering of God. Our church was filled with my favorite color, Pink. Hot pink, light pink, and a little bit of black splashed in to make the church look elegant and gorgeous. I had the traditional white wedding dress. The guys were all dressed in their black tuxes with a hot pink vest. Conner and Colton had on black slacks, with a white dress shirt and a hot pink tie. They both looked so handsome. I had Conner and Colton walk me down the aisle. I met my dad at the front so he could give me away. Merging our two families included Kris and Adam. There were two front-row seats with bundles of flowers reserved in memory of Kris and Adam.

Before the wedding started, we made a unity jar representing everyone involved. We took a crystal vase and put rocks in the bottom from the beach where Robbin proposed. Each family member put in an item that represented them. Robbin put in a Yankee ball, a pink cross for me, a shark for Colton. Choc put a superman in for Conner, dad placed a spiderman in for Adam and Kris's sister, Tracy, placed a superman golf ball in for Kris. Pastor Todd put a card with the scripture Matthew 6:33 written on it. The unity jar sits in our living room as a reminder of the family we merged that day.

The vows were read. We said *I do*. Robbin kissed his bride, and I danced down the aisle to the song "Walking on Sunshine". All the while holding the hand of the man that brought my heart back to life. There was a horse-drawn carriage waiting outside the church, like a fairy tale, my Prince helped me into the carriage, and we rode off into the sunset. The carriage took us a couple of blocks to a local venue where our reception was held. When we pulled up and got out of the carriage, Choc was waiting on us with a shotgun. He acted like he was after Robbin for marrying me. It was very funny.

We had music so everyone could dance and enjoy themselves. I talked Robbin into doing a fun dance for our first dance as a married couple. We took small tracks of several songs and made dance moves for each track. Anyone who knows Robbin knows he does not like to be in the spotlight at all. It took a lot of convincing to get him to agree. Our friend Darah was the only one who knew about it. She helped us work out the dance moves. We wanted to surprise everyone. It turned out awesome and entertaining. It was one of the highlights of the evening!

Grateful for our friends David and Marla, they graciously paid for us to go to Maui for our honeymoon. Talk about starting our marriage off in paradise. I kept pinching myself to make sure I wasn't dreaming! To have just had a beautiful wedding and then spending six nights in paradise was like a dream come true. It was what we needed. Spending several days alone together before coming back to reality.

With Conner being on a ventilator, we run a twenty-four-hour ICU out of our home. I wouldn't have it any other way. I knew our marriage was going to be a lot different than mine and Kris's. I knew somehow God would work it all out, because this was his plan.

We are beyond blessed. Our family steps up to the plate to help with Conner. Every year they encourage us to get away, even if it is just for a couple of days or sometimes for more extended periods. They know that we need to have some alone and downtime together. Robbin's mom, Pam, is a nurse and had been helping with Conner. My mom went to nursing school and got her LPN license. With all the issues we had with nursing in the beginning, it was nice to finally have a couple of nurses who were as devoted to Conner as we were.

I think about how truly blessed I am that God placed Robbin in my life. There probably aren't many men that would step into the role as he did with Conner. Stepping up in such a way shows the character of the man he truly is. The complex medical needs never mattered, and to see the father Robbin is, is truly unique. If you didn't know our story, you would think he was Conner's birth father! When we are out, it never fails, someone always walks up to say hi to Conner. They look at Robbin and say, "Your son looks just like you!" Robbin always smiles really big, looks over at me and winks, and then says, "I know!"

I won't say that things have always been easy. Getting to see Adam's friends grow up and be around them was a blessing for me. They still remembered Adam and made sure to let me know that. Conner getting to go to the sporting events of Colton and Adam's friends was a blessing. Getting to watch one of Adam's best friends Cole grow up, play sports, and walk across the graduation stage made my heart happy! I wouldn't have gotten to be a part of all these things if it wasn't for Colton being in the same grade as Adam. All of Adam's friends embraced Conner and always went out of their way to love on him. Even though Colton being in the same grade as Adam was hard at times, it was a blessing. God let me experience things I wouldn't have been able to experience if he wouldn't have come into my life. By no means can anyone replace Adam, but God gave me a blessing through Colton. I know he isn't my blood, but I love him just like he is! I am honored to be his bonus mom!

Making it Possible

I knew we would need help from insurance to cover the therapy's cost at the **Kennedy Krieger Institute**. Even continuing to do fundraisers, with the therapy's cost and our cost of living there, is very expensive.

I contacted Pat Ownbey, our local State Representative. Our families belonged to the same church. Pat helped me navigate getting our State Insurance to cover the Kennedy Krieger Institute. I didn't have any of the connections at our State Insurance agency to get anywhere. This was more than merely submitting a request.

Pat, who wasn't in our district, really stepped up to the plate. He got meetings set up with the CEO of our State Health Insurance Agency and several other higher up people in the agency. We had issues with some of his medical supplies not being covered. With that said, we do pay for a lot of supplies out of pocket, and there are some items that only a direct medical company can buy.

I was a nervous wreck as Pat, Robbin and I walk into the building. I wasn't sure how the meeting was going to go. Lisa Gifford met us at the door. She introduced herself and led us into the meeting room. As we were sat at a conference table, more and more people kept coming in. Everyone introduced themselves and found a seat. One of the men we met was Nico Gomez. Nico and Lisa would become strong advocates for Conner and friends. As they gave me the floor to voice my issues and concerns, I looked in their eyes and could tell they cared. It made a huge difference in getting to talk to them and telling our story from the beginning. I made it clear that as Conner's mother, I had to do everything in my power to give him the best possibility for a future.

Keeping him healthy would save them money in the long run. It would also cut down on hospital stays. I also voiced my concerns about some of our supplies. One of the supplies we were concerned with was Conner's mickey extenders. Mickey extenders are used to connect the feeding pump to Conner's G-Tube in his stomach. We only get four a month. The recommended cleaning procedure was to rinse them with water then soak them in vinegar. I had brought one that we had "cleaned" to the meeting. I pulled it out of my purse and showed it to them. I asked if anyone wanted to use it as a straw to drink their water. Of course, they all said no. Would they let their child eat off of a dirty plate? I felt like my son was. We continued the meeting like this, showing the health officials some of the struggles we dealt with and some solutions we had come up with.

After the meeting, the agency agreed to pay for the therapy cost at the Kennedy Krieger Institute. So often, insurance companies only see a number and not a person. From here on out, they saw Conner, not a number when issues arose along our journey. I was passionate, and I wasn't going to take no for an answer. This was all new territory for me and the beginning of the path of becoming an advocate for disabled children. I am now on a Members Advisory Task Force board for our state insurance as a parent of a special needs child. I'm also on another Advisory Committee for people with developmental disabilities.

We continue doing fundraisers to help with the cost of living expenses on our trips to Baltimore and the medical supplies that aren't covered. We have the most amazing community. When there is a need, our community steps up to the plate. One of our biggest fundraisers has been our "Run Because You Can" 5K and one mile fun run. We have several friends dress up as superhero's and run the race. We encourage everyone to come dressed as their favorite superhero. At every race, several people wear one of Conner's super "C" shirts and tell us they are dressed up as Conner, their favorite superhero. Erin always pushes Conner in this race. Erin loves to run , and it was always her dream to push Conner in a 5K. When we decided to start the run as a fundraiser, she was excited. Conner loves it! It lets him feel like he is getting to be a part of the run along with everyone else. Robbin had to do some engineering to his special needs jogging stroller, but he never fails to adapt things for Conner.

As we continue our journey to the Kennedy Krieger Institute, we have watched Conner grow and accomplish so much. They send all of his medical records to our neurosurgeon and our primary care physician. Our neurosurgeon, Dr. Wellington, had a complete change of heart watching Conner over the years and reading his reports from the **Kennedy Krieger Institute**. He told me he was glad I chose to go on with Conner's life even though they were all against it initially. He told us every time he sees a spinal cord injury patient now, he thinks of Conner and never says never. We have formed a great relationship over the years. He tells us seeing Conner at his yearly appointments is always the highlight of his year. He sees the miracle in Conner. He told us he expected within the first year for his extremities to be drawn up like a pretzel. Dr. Wellington even recommended Conner a "Make A Wish" to Disney World.

The Make a Wish Foundation had us fly on a commercial airline. Walking into the airport, we had four luggage carts full of luggage and all of Conner's medical supplies. Getting through security was an adventure in itself with all of Conner's medical equipment. After finally getting through security, we made our way to the plane. The pilots and flight attendants went above and beyond to help us. Most of Conner's medical equipment and supplies can't go underneath the plane. They let us board thirty minutes before anyone else. We were able to figure out where to put all of his equipment and supplies. Commercial airlines do not have a place for a wheelchair to sit inside the plane. Conner had to sit in an actual seat. As a quadriplegic, this isn't an easy task. Luckily Conner was young. If he had been older, this would have been an impossible task in a regular airline seat.

We accomplished a commercial plane ride going and coming back home. Conner and our family had a fantastic time at Disney World. We went in the fall, and there were hardly any lines for the rides. Disney World has many rides that are wheelchair accessible. For the first time since the accident, I got to see my little boy enjoy things other kids were getting to do. One of his favorite rides was the Toy Story ride at Hollywood Studios. We had to ride it over and over because he loved it so much. The characters and workers at the Disney Parks go above and beyond to make special needs kids feel like they are really special. It was a trip of a lifetime for Conner to get to experience.

One of the days we were there, we decided to go to Cocoa Beach, where the space shuttle takes off. Drum roll to another crazy adventure. During the drive back, Colton was tired and cranky and was being a brat. Robbin had got on to him, and he was pouting. When we got to the hotel, Robbin was having a "talk" with Colton as he was getting Conner out of the car. He didn't hear me tell him that Conner was still hooked up to his feeding pump. Robbin picked up Conner and his vent and turned to head inside. Conner's G-Tube was pulled out of him with the balloon inflated. We all panicked. The G-Tube is changed monthly. It has a balloon that keeps it in place. When changing the G-tube, you deflate the balloon. Because we were unsure of the trauma it might have caused, I used a sterile medical Q-tip to keep the hole in his stomach open. We piled back into the car and made a mad dash to the closest children's hospital.

Mom got on the phone and called everyone on her list, one by one, asking them to pray for Conner. Mom wasn't giving any explanation as to why he needed prayer. She was just saying pray for Conner and then hanging up. Mom had everyone in Ardmore on their knees, praying. Colton was in the back seat crying his eyes out, repeating over and over that he killed Conner. I was trying my best to hold Conner, keep the Q-tip positioned while attempting to console Colton, and assure him that Conner wasn't going to die. We called ahead to tell the hospital we were coming and what happened. They told us they would be waiting for us. Our fear was that hole in Conner's stomach may close up if we take too long, or he might need surgery to fix any trauma.

Robbin drove like a madman. We all believed he was in serious condition. I was holding Conner, keeping myself calm and consoling Colton. We flew up into the ER entrance like a racecar driver slides into the pit. Robbin jumps out, grabs Conner and we all rush inside. We expected it to be a scene like you see in the movies where doctors and nurses come running out with a gurney to meet and rush you in. Nope, nothing like that. We were all breathing hard and in a complete panic. Standing in the empty waiting room for what seemed like an hour (in reality, it was probably less than a minute), one nurse comes calmly walking out. The nurse asked if we were the family of the child with a removed G-Tube? I said *yes* and showed her Conners belly where the Q-tip was lodged. The nurse took us back into one of the rooms. While she was looking over his stomach, she asked if we had brought Conners back up G-tube. We handed it to her. She opens the package, preps the G-tube, and inserts it into Conner's belly. I know all of our jaws must have dropped at the same time. The nurse looks at us and smiles, she said, *Don't worry, this happens all the time, is there anything else we can help you with?* We all got back in the car and started laughing.

After that amazing epic vacation, we realized that commercial flights would not be an option the older and bigger Conner got. One day I'm going to make it my mission to make commercial airlines wheelchair accessible. We know it's a blessing that we can fly to Baltimore on a private jet. Our local organization flew us twice. For the rest of our trips, we fly privately with an anonymous donor who is like family. When flying to Baltimore, we have to pack two week's worth of supplies and equipment. The plane is always packed full. The pilots are always so gracious loading and unloading the plane. They always go above and beyond and will never know how much we appreciate them.

Breathing On His Own

Cleveland, Ohio

We started noticing Conner breathing on his own as we carried him from room to room. When we move him, we take him entirely off of the ventilator. It's easier to move him this way. One day, we decided to leave him off the ventilator for a few more minutes after moving him to see how long he could go. Conner began going longer and longer off of the vent. We realized that if we kept him entertained and not thinking about being off the ventilator, he started staying off for more extended periods. We got very creative. Mom would dress up as a clown, we would turn the music on loud and dance for him, Choc would rock him, and mom would make up silly songs about Conner. He loved every minute of it, and we did our job by keeping him occupied. He got up to two hours being off of the ventilator. I will never forget when Conner reached the two-hour mark, mom looked at me and asked, *What we do now*? He seemed perfectly content and in no distress. I told her I don't know, let's put him back on the vent. I wasn't sure what to do. What a blessing as I was told he would never be able to even take one breath on his own. Psalm 46:10 *Be still and know that I am God.*

The Kennedy Krieger Institute recommended that we check into a Doctor in Cleveland, Ohio, that was doing diaphragmatic pacers. Dr. Onders was having great success with patients being able to come off the ventilator. Robbin and I decided to go to the University Hospitals in Cleveland and talk with him about the diaphragmatic pacers. We would see if we felt comfortable with the procedure. Dr. Onders explained that he couldn't guarantee Conner would be a candidate. First, he had to see if his diaphragm was working. If the diaphragm was paralyzed, which in all honesty it should be, it wouldn't work. Dr. Onders explained how the pacers worked. He would place four wires in Conner's diaphragm, two on the left side and two on the right side. He then would run the wires up through his chest cavity, and they would come out just below his right clavicle. There is an external device that attaches to the wires to activate them. The pacers stimulate the diaphragm to strengthen it. It produces a more normal way of breathing.

A ventilator only works in the top part of the lungs. This is why so many people have issues with pneumonia while they are on a ventilator. The vent doesn't work in the bottom part of the lungs.

When we got back home, we asked our family, and I also reached out to our pastor to be praying about this. I am always cautious about what we do to Conner. I don't want to make a wrong decision that would negatively affect his life. After much prayer, we felt like God was leading us down this path. I got with the insurance to get it approved. In December 2011, we flew privately into Cleveland during a massive snowstorm to get the pacers placed. I think that was the most beautiful snow I had ever seen. They are so prepared for the snow in Cleveland. They keep the roads and sidewalks clear day and night.

My parents and stepparents all flew commercial. Robbin and I left out one little factor to my parents. Conner was going to be only the fourteenth pediatric patient to have this procedure. The doctor had done lots of adults but was just getting started on pediatrics because it's harder to get things approved for pediatrics in the US. We were hoping they wouldn't find out about this little bit of information. Mom tends to freak out with details like that sometimes. She worries about Conner. I thought we were in the clear until the very last minute, mom asked the Nurse Practitioner, Mary Jo how many of these procedures had they done. When Mary Jo said Conner was number fourteen, I thought my mom was going to pass out. I should have prepped the Mary Jo beforehand in case she asked.

As they took Conner back, I prayed that his diaphragm was working correctly. I had a feeling it was. How else would he be able to go two hours off the vent? I was scared. I knew if the Dr. Onders came out and said the diaphragm was paralyzed, there was no hope for Conner to ever get off the ventilator. That would have devastated me. I wanted more than anything for Conner to be able to get rid of the ventilator. I felt like it was a chain he was tied to. It took longer than the doctor said it would. I got nervous and anxious. We were the last ones in the waiting room. It was the end of the day. As the Dr. Onders comes out, he is excited.

He tells us that Conner's diaphragm is working and was in fact, beautiful and strong. He was amazed to see that his diaphragm was in such good shape. We were all crying and thanking God for another miracle.

After Conner's procedure, we had a couple of days that we could explore. When we see snow in southern Oklahoma, it is usually a light dusting and gone by the next day. Cleveland got three feet of snow overnight. When we looked out the hotel window, we were amazed to see the streets were clean. The adventurist group we are, we decided to drive around and see all the beautiful snow and scenery. We found a beautiful old cemetery and a park that stretched for miles. My husband decided he wanted to make a snow angel in the park. To be fair, I wanted to make one too. We got out of the car and I was bundled up like a smart person. Robbin was in his signature khaki shorts and hoodie. Here he was, making snow angels in three foot of snow in his shorts. We got lots of strange looks, but we got a kick out of it.

Back home, we had gotten Conner off the vent for up to seven hours with the pacers. I need to push harder. Dr. Longhorn, Conner's pulmonologist, is always getting on to me for Conner not being off the ventilator more with the pacers. He told me one time, you take him all over the US for the best medical care. Then with the pacers, you come home and move at a snail speed with them. I think I am just as much addicted to the ventilator as Conner. Maybe even more. I am used to the sound the ventilator makes. It is an eerie sound when the ventilator is turned off. It is very quiet. I constantly worry and want to make sure that he is breathing okay when on his pacers. When Conner looks at me and gives me his big smile, I know he is okay. He likes being on them. I think it is because Conner is getting a better breath than he does on the ventilator. He does tire out after a while on them, as this is exercising his diaphragm. Even moving at a snail speed, we will eventually get there on being off the ventilator all day.

More Adventures

We make it a mission to go on family trips and let Conner see the world. We don't want a wheelchair to define his life. We live life to the fullest. When we are done with therapy, we do a lot of sightseeing around Baltimore. There is so much history within driving distance. Since we have the weekends off from therapy, sometimes we take longer trips. Conner got to go to New York City and tour the old Yankee Stadium the last weekend they were doing tours. Robbin has always been a Yankee fan and turned Conner into one too. Walking through the stadium was a special moment for Robbin. He was on cloud nine. Since Conner and another gentlemen were in wheelchairs, we couldn't do the regular tour with all the other people. It involved stairs. We got our own private tour and got to walk down the halls that Babe Ruth and Derek Jeter walked. The other group of people didn't get to walk the same halls.

Conner got to see Times Square and the Empire State building. We may have had him out a little too late that night. We were eating pizza slices at 1 am. It was almost 2 am when we were on the subway heading back to our hotel. He loved every minute of it. Times Square is pretty entertaining at night and mesmerizing with all of the lights.

We love to take Conner to sporting events. College football games are his favorite. Of course, being from Oklahoma, OU is his favorite team. I think the football games are his favorite because our seats are right in front of the cheerleaders. We have taken him to several major league baseball games as well. It seems like every time we are in Baltimore in May. The Orioles are playing the Yankees. So, you know what that means. We're not going to pass up the opportunity to see the Yankees play.

The beach is one of our favorite family trips. There is nothing more relaxing than the sound of the waves crashing on the beach. Conner could sit on the balcony for hours listening to that sound. These vacations are more laid back and not going all the time to see sights. I don't know how you could ever get tired of watching and listening to the waves crash on the beach. It is my happy place, as well.

Conner has been turkey hunting with daddy Robbin, but they never got the turkeys close enough to kill one. Conner had fun dressing up in his camo and sitting inside the tent. Robbin built an "all-terrain" wagon so he could get Conner into the woods. Conner couldn't stop chuckling when they called the turkeys up. This may be why the turkeys didn't get close enough to shoot.

There are no limitations when it comes to the things I tell Robbin I want to do. I want life to be as normal as it can be for Conner. The bigger he has gotten makes it a little more complicated to travel with him, but that doesn't stop us. Robbin always figures out a way. Luckily, Colton is a big stout boy. That comes in handy for helping with Conner's lifting. We have a routine down as a family when we go on trips. We have to take all of Conner's medical supplies and back up of things in case something went wrong. I always say we pack the whole house except for the kitchen sink. It takes a lot of work and preparation to go on trips, but it is worth it. I am thankful our family works together. I can't imagine Conner only experiencing life stuck in the house all the time. That would be depressing to me, and I am sure to Conner as well.

One of my favorite adventures is our big family trip to Yellowstone a couple of years ago. We took two RV's. Dad took his RV, and we rented one from my cousin. Mom and Katrina's family joined this adventure. While in the park, we decided that we wanted Conner to see an incredible waterfall. It was supposed to have a handicap accessible trail. I'm not sure who classified this trail as handicap accessible. It was a steep and bumpy switchback dirt trail with no railing except on a couple of corners. If you lost your footing, you would go off the side of the mountain. A lot of the people we passed, while going down the trail, were in shock. They kept commenting that they struggled going down and couldn't believe we were taking a wheelchair down. I was getting a little nervous, but Robbin and Colton assured me they had it all under control. They were determined to get him down. Robbin's legs were cramping by the time we got to the waterfall. Conner laughed the whole way down. The rougher, the better for him. He is all boy.

I was relieved when we got down to the bottom!! I think I held my breath most of the way down, praying they didn't lose their footing. What a beautiful sight to see when we got to the waterfall! I was happy Conner was getting to see it. Conner loved sitting and watching the water rush over the fall! The waterfall was rushing into what looked like the Grand Canyon. Even with the loud sound of flowing water, it was also a peaceful sound. God's beauty is beyond amazing!

Time to go back up the mountain. I knew the climb wasn't going to be easy. The only way they could get momentum to get up the mountain was for Colton to run while pushing Conner up the hill. We were in a loose dirt trail I mind you, and I was panicking. Knowing that if he lost his footing, Conner would go off the side of the cliff. The guys had a system. Colton was pushing in the back, and Robbin was in front, pulling the wheelchair. The rest of my family was trying to be a barrier in case Colton did lose his footing. I was getting nervous watching them. I told my sister to go on up with them, and I would stay behind with my parents. My parents weren't moving up the hill as fast as everyone else. Conner thought this was very comical, watching my family work together to get him up the cliff. He laughed the whole way back up the mountain, as everyone else was about to pass out from all the hard work. I decided to hang back a little because I was so nervous.

When they got close to the top, Robbin and Colton's legs gave out on them. Two college boys from Texas were going down the hill and asked if they could help get Conner the rest of the way to the top. It was a God thing they came along at the moment, Robbin and Colton were exhausted. The two college boys finished pushing Conner up the hill. Even as hard as it was on Robbin and Colton to get Conner down to the waterfall and back up, they both said they would do it all over again for Conner to experience it. That is what I love about our family! There are no limitations for letting Conner experience the world.

Birthday Gift

On my thirty-sixth birthday, mom gave me the best surprise birthday gift! She orchestrated and did a lot of planning to make this memorable for me. When I woke up, she told me I needed to head over to Robbin's shop, where his business is located. When I walked into the shop, she had my senior prom dress, makeup, and all my hair stuff waiting for me. She told me to get all dolled up and wait for further instructions. I thought there was no way I could squeeze into this form-fitting long green sequence dress. Thankfully the dress had stretchy material. After letting her know I was all dolled up and ready, Choc drove over to the shop to pick me up. As I walked into the living room, mom told me that Conner had a big surprise for me. She made me turn away from the door going into Conner's therapy room and asked me to close my eyes. We have a lift system in the ceiling that goes all the way through Conner's bedroom, into his therapy room and into the living room.

I could hear them doing something with the lift system, I assumed Conner was on it. My mom told me I could open my eyes and turn around. When I turned around, I saw Conner dressed so handsome in a suit and top hat. Mom had put Conner in his harness that we use to walk him on the treadmill. This way, he was in a standing position. As the song "I hope you dance" starts playing, my heart was overjoyed as I was going to dance with my little boy for the first time after the accident. As Conner and I danced to the song, I sang to him. He had the biggest smile on his face, so did I. It's the little things I took for granted in life before. On that birthday, I was on cloud nine dancing with my sweet little boy!

Adam's Cape

It is incredible to look back over the last fourteen years and see how God had my life lined up for all the things that would take place. Even though I have had many heartaches, God has blessed me double fold as well. I would love for Conner to be up walking right now and not experiencing this life of a spinal cord injury! I know that if that were the case, we wouldn't have witnessed firsthand the miracles God has done in our lives. For some reason, this is God's plan for our lives. We have to keep moving forward. I have to remind myself daily that God is in control and wants the best for us.

As a family, we decided we wanted to help other families going through medical crises or needing medical equipment. Our community has been so faithful at giving to us through all of our local fundraisers. We know firsthand what it is like to need specialized treatment or a piece of expensive medical equipment that insurance won't cover. We all prayed about it and decided we wanted to start a non-profit called Adam's Cape. Adam's Cape mission is to provide support and services to children with medical needs or crisis. We have eleven board members. Our board members have caring hearts and a passion for helping children. Over the years, we have been able to help several children and pray we can help thousands more in the future. Starting a nonprofit has been such a blessing and a great way to honor Adam and Kris. The cape in Adam's Cape represents Kris since he was such a big Superman fan.

A letter to me

If I could write a letter now and somehow get it to myself back when the accident happened, it would be this.

Sonya,

You are about to go through a horrific tragedy in your life! It will be more challenging than you could ever imagine! You will experience many days that the pain is so unbearable that it hurts even to breathe! There will be numerous days that you wish it was you who was in the wreck and not Kris. You would much rather be in heaven than here enduring the pain you are experiencing. There are many days you will feel like you aren't strong enough for this journey you are traveling, but I want you to know that you are stronger than you could ever imagine!

Remember that the power of prayer is the most powerful tool you have on your side! God loves you and has not forsaken you! Don't worry about tomorrow, because tomorrow doesn't exist yet. We only have today! A quote mom will tell you a lot over the years.

I know that you think you will never find true love again, laugh again, or experience real joy again! I promise you will. Keep your heart open! Let God work in yours and Conner's life! I promise he has BIG plans for your life!

You are going to be physical, emotionally, and mentally exhausted! You will basically be running a twenty-four-hour ICU out of your home, but the reward of seeing Conner so happy and continually making progress is going to be worth every minute of it. Coming home and dealing with Kris and Adam's loss will take a significant toll on you emotionally and physically. You long for them and feel like you will never get over the heartache. I promise you do start healing your broken heart! The pain is always there, but you find joy and happiness again.

Always continue to let Conner experience life to the fullest! You are a great mom, and you always make sure he gets to live life like any other child! You will make sure Conner gets to see the world, and never stop doing that! He will love getting to go and getting out of the house! Conner will always have such a deep trust for you and a bond between the two of you that is unbreakable. He loves you deeply. You can see it in his eyes when he looks at you.

You will take him several states away to ensure he gets the highest level of care and therapy for his injury. You continue to push him and work with him at home. Conner is a fighter and is strong. Stronger than you can even imagine. The word Hope becomes a common household word in your home! You will have to make many medical decisions in your life for Conner and learn more than you ever dreamed of when it comes to medical issues. You will always pray about it and make sure you are doing the right thing for Conner! Trust me, you know him better than any other human being. Don't ever doubt yourself when it comes to his medical conditions. Conner always has a smile on his face and trust you. He is truly a precious child of God!

An amazing man is going to be brought into your life. His name is Robbin! God has been preparing your heart for this ever since the accident happened. God has been preparing your heart for all of this since the moment you were conceived. You will want to close your heart off at first because it feels like you are cheating on Kris. Trust me. You will find room for both of them in your heart!

Robbin will grasp you and Conner right into the palm of his hands. If you didn't know your story, you would never know that Conner wasn't his own blood. It takes a Godly and loving man to fill these shoes. You are also going to bring so much happiness that he has been longing for in a marriage. You are both true blessings to each other. You will show his son and Conner what a Godly marriage looks like!

Always be honest with him about what you are going through. Tell him when you need a moment to yourself to grieve. Always work together as husband and wife. This makes life much easier when the two of you split the daily and nightly tasks with Conner. You don't get many nights of uninterrupted sleep because you have to cath Conner and change his position at 3:00 am every night. Robbin will help you by doing these nightly tasks on the weekends. His help will give you much-needed sleep three nights a week. He will take the place of family and friends who helped you until you got married, with night shift duty. Even though you think you can do it all on your own, you are very stubborn. Trust me. You need the help!

Working together is very rewarding and grows your marriage much stronger! Many married couples who have children with disabilities end up divorced or co-existing in the same house with no relationship. You won't be one of those statics. You two will have a strong, loving, and Godly marriage.

Every night at bedtime will be Conner's highlight of the day. He will laugh at the two of you multi-tasking doing his breathing treatments, getting his nightly feed together, cathing him, and arguing (in a fun way) who positions him better on his side for bed. Conner loves it when you play song quiz on Alexa. You will quickly realize music is always something Conner will love! Conner will just laugh and love every second of it. This thirty-minute bedtime adventure would take you almost an hour if you didn't have help.

You are blessed to have the family and friend support that you have. Always be grateful for them all because they never leave your side through this "New Normal" journey you are on. They love you and Conner! They are with you every step of the way!

Trust me when I say that God truly blesses you and numerous others through Conner! Conner is the glue that gives you a reason to live and hope that you will smile and laugh again! Conner always pushes hard to overcome what has happened to him and continually does it with a smile on his face. Your little boy loves you so much and needs you just as much as you need him. God knew what he was doing when he placed that sweet little boy in your womb! Conner is a fighter and a survivor just like you are!

Keep trusting God and keep pushing through this life! You become a great advocate for other families going through trials like you! You get to be a voice for all the other Conner's in Oklahoma! The strong-willed, hard-headed little girl you are growing up will turn into a brave, stubborn, hard-head that will move mountains. You will become an example for people in all walks of life. You got this!! #FaithOverFear

Sonya

Final thoughts

When you are running a race, you cannot get distracted by what you see along the route. You have to picture the finish line and run as hard as you can until you get there. The Bible reminds us in Philippians 3:13, *"But one thing I do: Forgetting what is behind and straining toward what is ahead."* I cannot go back and change the past, as much as I would like to some days. What I can do is choose hope instead of despair, even in the moments the weight of what I have lost wants to crash over me. I can fix my eyes on Jesus. As long as I am focused on Him, I can keep going.

Questions For Brooke, Our Physical Therapist

1. The first time you worked with Conner, what were your thoughts about him?

The first time I worked with Conner, I was first drawn to his smile that absolutely lights up his face! Once I got to know Conner during our first time working together, I was struck by what a hard worker he was, despite being so young and having gone through so much trauma. He always had smiles for me, no matter how hard I was making him work! I also very quickly learned how smart and aware he was, despite being non-verbal and limited in his movement.

2. After 13 years of working with Conner as his Physical Therapist at Kennedy Krieger Institute, what are some of the biggest changes you have seen in him?

The biggest changes I've seen in Conner functionally are his ability to interact with his environment, his ability to hold his head up by himself, increased independence with sitting, and increased movement in his shoulders and arms. The biggest impact I've seen in terms of his health and quality of life are related to how healthy he's been with limited medical complications.

3. What are some health issues you would have expected to see arise with Conner throughout the years due to his spinal cord injury, that haven't happened so far?

There are many health issues I would have expected to see in Conner based on how young he was injured, his high cervical level injury, and being on a ventilator. Two of the biggest, potentially life-threatening complications are pneumonia and pressure wounds, which he has never had. This is amazing for an individual with any spinal cord injury, and especially for Conner because his injury was so involved. There are several other secondary effects of paralysis that are common that Conner has not experienced, including pathological fracture of his bones, blood clots, and surgical correction of scoliosis. Additionally, there are multiple complications that are very common in patients with spinal cord injury, that Conner has experienced at a lower frequency or severity than expected, including joint contractures and urinary tract infections.

4. What are your thoughts about Conner's mom?

Sonya is truly amazing. I look up to her for so many reasons. The care she provides to Conner is exceptional. The fact that he's remained so active and healthy since his accident is a true testament to her love and care. Sonya is diligent in ensuring she understands the care, equipment, and therapy activities recommended for Conner and carries them out consistently. Her knowledge of the medical management of spinal cord injury, physical therapy, occupational therapy, and Conner's specific needs is incredible. She makes balancing his many medical needs, every day personal care needs, and therapy needs look easy. She loves and protects him fiercely, and goes above and beyond to ensure Conner gets to experience many adventures in life, from elaborate birthday celebrations, creative adapted Halloween costumes, to travelling and vacations.

She is also an amazing advocate for Conner. Sonya will never back down from going after the things Conner needs to be successful and healthy in life. Not only does she advocate for Conner, but she serves as a strong advocate for others with disabilities in Oklahoma.

5. Do you feel like Conner has the drive and determination to want to do things?

Yes! When he was younger, the key was to find toys to motivate him to do tasks, which is true of any kid! As he's gotten older, he's very easy going and participates in pretty much whatever you ask of him! He is a hard worker and the smile and pride on Conner's face when he accomplishes something is clear.

6. Do you believe the specialized spinal cord injury therapy Conner gets at Kennedy Krieger Institute is a big contributor to his overall health?

Yes, I do. I believe that the specialized activity-based therapy and medical care he receives twice a year at Kennedy Krieger, which is then carried over at home by his family, has been a huge contributor to his overall health and quality of life. At the International Center for Spinal Cord Injury, we're able to provide specific therapy recommendations, education for his family, and equipment recommendations to be carried out at home on a long-term basis in order to optimize his function, as well as keep him healthy and prevent secondary complications of paralysis. This leads to decreased sick time, decreased need for medications and medical interventions, and decreased hospitalizations- which overall lead to an improved quality of life for Conner.

Letters From Friends

Darah Crouch

It is hard to even know where to begin talking about my precious friend Sonya and her family. Their family has become a regular topic when I share the gospel with people where I work. People often think they have experienced the worst, or they are in the worst situation currently. I then share how my friend lost everything as she knew it in one day, but she has chosen to glorify God in her circumstances continually.

When she texted me to see if I could jot down some early memories, I began to cry, thinking about the day of the accident so freshly and what I would share. I think of it often. It isn't something you can watch someone go through and not be changed by it. I was sick and shocked when I got the phone call. It seemed impossible. I had just seen Kris playing with the boys in the church foyer as they were headed out to Mother's Day lunch. We all were laughing and saying our typical "see ya laters". Kris and Adam were so full of life. We were all so young. I didn't even know how to be a friend in such devastating times. I just knew I needed to go. Every time I hear the song "Bad Day," it takes me back to that day in the hospital at Dallas. It was a popular song, and someone's ring tone kept going off playing it in the middle of everything. It can still feel so fresh, like it was just yesterday.

I will never forget Sonya's face and the pain in her eyes. Being a mom, I just couldn't fathom what she had to process. Not only was she fighting for her son's life, but she also had a husband and a son, she had to go burry. She had to see their caskets in a place that was once saturated in joy. Those days were devastating. The most I knew to do was make sure I could relieve any burden possible when around at the hospital or help with things at home. A situation like this could ruin a person, but it didn't. I was amazed by her! From the beginning, she relentlessly protected Conner, sought wise counsel, and left his life in God's hands. She was always by his side. I remember watching how tired she and her mom were, but they chose to smile, laugh and uplift Conner daily. Every day was a fight for his life. She could have easily given up with it just being too much to bear. It is certainly not too much for our God, and when she was empty and at the end, she cried out to her Father that continued to carry and sustain her.

Through Conner's life, the Lord has brought so many people to Himself. It was amazing to me watching Sonya and her family look to share Christ with everyone along the way. Whether it was doctors, nurses, other patients, people placed in their path, they decided to share Christ and have their gospel tracts ready. I had grown up in church my entire life, but I was lost amid it all. I am confident the Lord used these circumstances to shake in me the reality of eternity. My brother was speaking truth into my life, the Lord was drawing me, and God made it impossible for me not to see His goodness in it all. I remember coming out to sleep in Conner's room one night so Sonya could get a good night's sleep. Conner would just sing the sweetest noises. It was as if the Lord was allowing him to see something none of the rest of us could. I had such peace in that room. I didn't have peace like that. I was restless talking a good church game, and I didn't come to know that peace until Christ broke through and saved me.

I learned from this family what it looks like to come together in hard times. I learned what it looks like to dance in the rain. That the enemy could not steal their laughter and joy even though somedays the pain would be so deep at times it was crippling. The Lord was their strength. I learned what it looks like for a mother to give up everything to be the mother God has called her to be. Sonya and I spent many nights talking and crying. I couldn't begin to imagine what it felt like to miss Kris and Adam the way she did. I see why the Lord tells us to keep our minds set on the things above and not on the things on earth. It's too much here at times, and it certainly was for my friend. Her strength and endurance amaze me. She fights for Conner to this day. She is better than any nurse that could ever work with him, and she has become more knowledgeable than most. She looks out for others along the path they have walked, not just trying to improve Conner's life, but she wants to help others that struggle taking care of children with special medical needs. Sonya was determined not only to let Conner survive. She exhausted herself, lifting, exercising, and motivating him. It was one of the biggest blessings to see my amazing and weary friend get a gift of a husband that loves her unconditionally and took Conner on as his own. There are too many stories to share along their journey, but Robbin is one of my favorite parts. I saw my friend smiling and enjoying life with a sweet man that the Lord sent. Sonya and Robbin have encouraged me in my hard times, and they are just a blessing to all who know them.

When I think back to watching Sonya slumping over hospital chairs to keep Conner comfortable or curled up next to that sweet baby in his bed, I see the faithfulness of God. He never left their side. When I remember us begging for Conner's life as different health situations arose, I see God's mercy as I look back at questioning why so much on this one family. I see how God has grown and changed me in trusting His sovereignty. None of this road has been in vain. I wish I could have changed it for them a million times, but I truly believe one day, when we are all standing in eternity, we will be glorifying God for what He has done here. We will understand what our small minds can't comprehend through the pain. I am forever grateful for the Lord putting this family in my life and using them as part of my sanctification.

Darah Crouch

Todd and Kim Davison

Our family moved to Ardmore, OK, in April of 2006. Todd had recently accepted a call to be the young adult pastor at First Baptist Church. We were from the Oklahoma City area and did not know anyone in Southern Oklahoma when we moved. Our oldest daughter was five years old, and our son was two at the time. We were still in the process of settling into our home and meeting many new faces at a church of around 800 people when the accident occurred involving the McDougall family. We had not had the opportunity to meet their family before the day of the wreck. Todd recalls being at the church when several people started calling in and letting the church know about the accident shortly after it happened. He did not know the family, and no one knew how bad the accident was yet. He just remembers meeting the senior pastor, Dr. Alton Fannin, at the hospital a few minutes after the calls came in.

In the emergency room, there were a lot of family already present when they arrived. He recalls when little Conner was brought in from the ambulance. Todd said, 'I recall the hospital being filled with doctors and nurses hurrying about and many people that I did not know. I didn't know who the family was, who was a friend, or even who Sonya was. I recall seeing a woman in complete turmoil with a group of people around her, and I assumed that it was Sonya. It was. I recall that the news began to start spreading in that waiting area that Kris and Adam had passed away, and they were not certain that Conner would survive."

Todd did not try to interact with the people there very much because they did not know who he was. He tucked himself away and called me while I was at home, unpacking, and taking care of our children. He was having difficulty holding it together, witnessing all that he saw in the hospital that day. I heard the sorrow in his voice and went to the kitchen, away from my kids, so that I could hear him. I remember feeling nauseous and overwhelmed at the news he was telling me. I looked in the other room at my own two children around the same age as these two brothers involved in the wreck. I was heartbroken for this mother.

160

My heart also went out to my husband, who was trying to remain strong in the midst of a grieving family. All I remember doing is praying and crying. I waited by the phone for any updates on Conner. Todd watched as they med flighted him out to Dallas.

Todd recalls that once in Dallas, when he went to visit along with the senior pastor, Sonya was told by the physicians there that she should turn off the machines and let Conner pass. Sonya contacted Dr. Fannin in tears, asking him what he thought she should do. He told her to fight for him and do whatever she feels God is leading her to do without letting the doctors persuade her either way. Little did anyone know what an impact the faith and love of this mother and the strength and determination of Conner would have on our community.

Todd and Kim Davison

PHOTOS

First Family - McDougall's

First Family - McDougall's

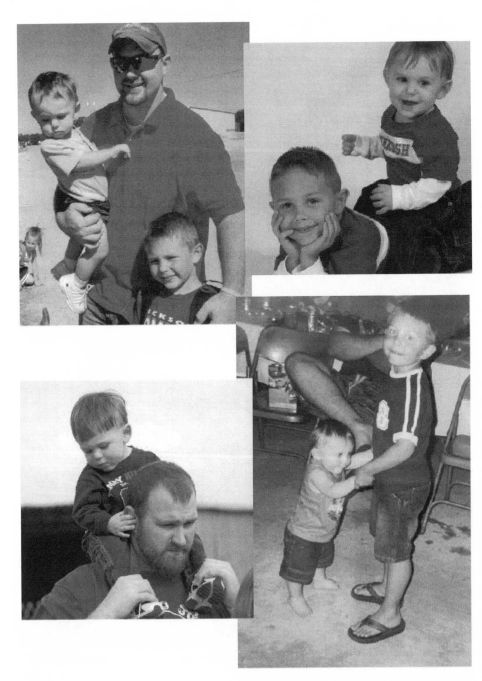

Wreck

ICU

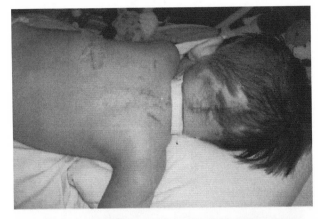

Spinal Fusion Scars

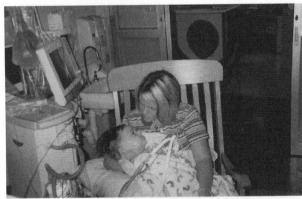

First Time to
Hold Conner
After Accident

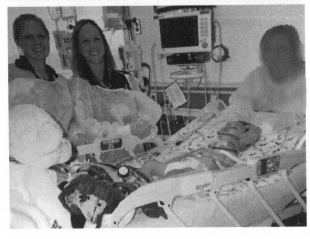

ICU Nurses

Conner Coming Home

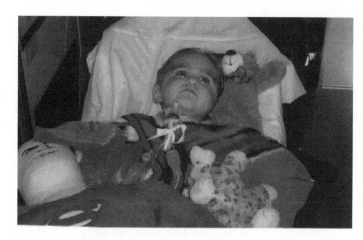

Ambulance
Bringing
Conner home

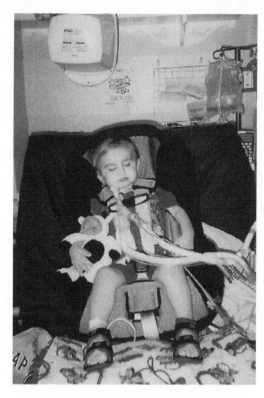

Conner asleep
in carseat I
bought to
show doctor
we didn't
need
ambulance
transportation

New Love

New Family - The Hunter's

Therapy

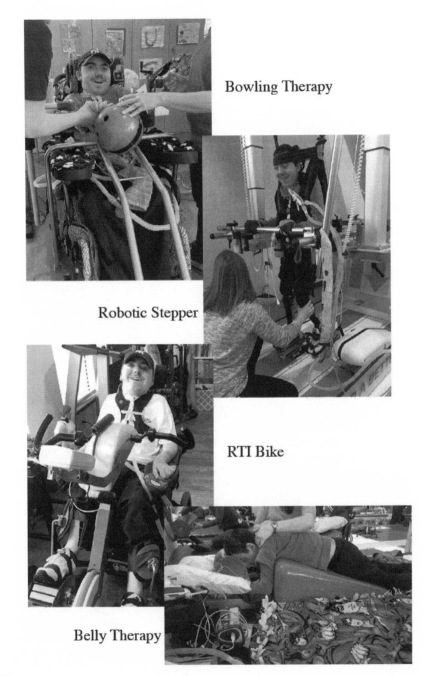

Bowling Therapy

Robotic Stepper

RTI Bike

Belly Therapy

Therapy

Conner's Families

Sonya's Family

Robbins Family

Kris's Family

Grandparent's

My mom and Stepdad Choc

My dad and Stepmom Donna

Robbin's
mom and Dad

Great Grandparents

My Grandma Butler

Kris's Grandma Lebo

Siblings

My Sister Katrina

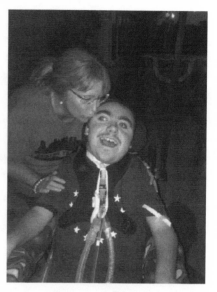

My Stepsister Tracy

My Stepsister Jennifer
and my nephew Andy

Kris's Siblings
Tracy, Jeff, Tony and Amanda

Halloween Costume

Darth Vader
Tie Fighter

Batman

The Red Baron

Monkey in Space

Monkey Boy

Run Because You Can 5K

Sporting Events

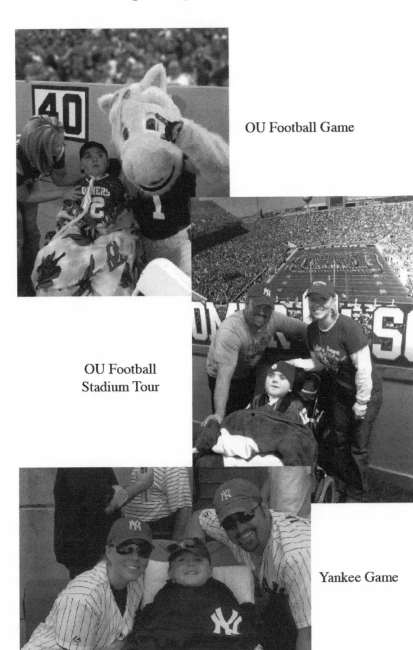

OU Football Game

OU Football
Stadium Tour

Yankee Game

Adventures

Christmas Lights

Turkey Hunting

Beach Time

Pappy and the Grands

Yellowstone Cliff

Adventures

Disney World
Toy Story Ride

Lincoln Memorial

Statue of Liberty

New York City

Arlington Cemetery

Conner

Conner

Conner

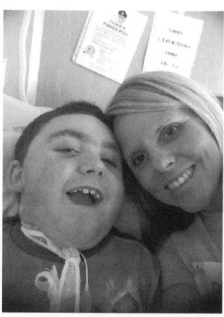

Conner

Pat Ownbey, Lisa Gifford, and Nico Gomez

39th Birthday Dance

Mommy Little Mister Dance

Acknowledgment

God is the most important thank you for this book! If it weren't for his loving grace, this book wouldn't be.

I am thankful for my parents Gail, the late Choc, Tim and Donna. If they hadn't raised me in a Christian home, I wouldn't have the faith that I have today. Thank you, guys, for always being my biggest cheerleader and never leaving my side!! I don't know how I would have faced this tragedy without all of you. Thank you for always stepping up to the plate once a year to keep Conner so Robbin and I can get away for a few days. Mom, thank you for quitting your job in the beginning and staying by my side through it all! I know you sacrificed a lot for us, and I will be forever grateful for that! Even though I know you didn't consider it a sacrifice. I am proud of you for getting your nurse's license through all of this! I love you all!

Thank you to my close friends for never leaving my side through all of this.

Thank you, Katrina, for helping us get this book completed. It was a family event to make my writings a masterpiece! You rocked it! I am thankful that God picked you to be my sister! I love you!

I am thankful for my husband, Robbin, and bonus son, Colton. You guys pushed me and encouraged me to complete this book! Robbin, thank you for being my rock! Thank you for stepping up to the plate of being Daddy Robbin to Conner. God blessed me, bringing you and Colton into my life. I love you both more than you will ever know!

Thank you, Dale and Pam, for raising your son to be a Godly man! Thank you, Pam, for always stepping in to help us take care of Conner! I am so thankful that you guys embraced Conner and me with loving arms into your family! We love you both!

Thank you, Monica Madden, for your coach writing with this book and your positive words of encouragement! I am thankful that God brought our paths together! You are now a part of our family! Much love to you!

Thank you to the Empowered Living Community and The John Maxwell Team. I have been inspired by all of you to pursue my dream of finishing this book and speaking about our story!

My heart is full of love and gratitude for each and every person who became the hands and feet of Jesus on May nineteenth, two thousand and six, and continue to be today. There are too many people to personally thank on this page that went above and beyond to take care of all our needs during this time. We love you all!

Philippians 1:3 *I thank my God upon every remembrance of you.*

ADDITIONAL RESOURCES AVAILABLE AT:

www.29elevenministries.com

If this book touched or inspired you, I would love for you to leave a review at Amazon.com

Facebook @ UnSurvivable
Instagram @ 29eleven_Ministries

sonya@29elevenministries.com

Recommendations

https://www.adamscape.org

https://www.kennedykrieger.org

https://www.faithandfamilybox.com

https://johnmaxwellteam.com

www.yourempowered.life

Made in the USA
Monee, IL
02 February 2021